Hey! What's My Number?

Also by Christopher Carosa...

A Pizza The Action

– Everything I Ever Learned About Business I Learned by Working in a Pizza Stand at the Erie County Fair

50 Hidden Gems of Greater Western New York

– A Handbook for Those Too Proud to Believe "Wide Right" and "No Goal" Define Us.

401(k) Fiduciary Solutions

– Expert Guidance for 401(k) Plan Sponsors on How to Effectively and Safely Manage Plan Compliance and Investments by Sharing the Fiduciary Burden with Experienced Professionals

Due Diligence

– The Individual Trustee's Guide to Selecting and Monitoring a Professional Money Manager

Hey! What's My Number?

How To Improve

The Odds *You* Will

Retire in Comfort

by

Christopher Carosa

Pandamensional Solutions, Inc.

Mendon, New York

Published by Pandamensional Solutions, Inc., Mendon, NY

Cover design by Catarina Lena Carosa

ISBN-10: 1938465032
ISBN-13: 978-1-938465-03-1

What Others Are Saying About Christopher Carosa's
Hey! What's My Number?

"Today's 401k education meeting process is a farce. There's simply too much to learn, with too little time. Chris Carosa has done for the 401k what Americans need — he's made the difficult easier. He's created something simple and attainable for the Average Joe/Jane."
> ➤ Richard Burke, Principal – Retirement Plan Consulting & Administration Practice, Burke Group, Rochester, New York

"I found the process Chris uses helpful, and, after going through it, our employees now realize their future is brighter than they thought."
> ➤ Carol Chowaniec, Accountant, Springville Mfg. Co., Springville, New York

"Chris Carosa cuts through the nonsense. In a world filled with cheap and often badly wrong advice, anyone serious about their financial health and retirement is lucky to have Chris on their side."
> ➤ Allen Greenberg, Editor, Retirement, BenefitsPro, Summit Professional Network, Denver, Colorado

"Nothing is more important regarding your money than knowing how much you have, where it is, and that you won't outlive it at retirement. Chris Carosa provides an easy to understand roadmap for all 401k participants to follow, regardless of investing experience, to plan for a secure and comfortable future."
> ➤ Tom Zgainer, CEO, America's Best 401k, Scottsdale, Arizona

"For the past several years I've been part of a five-person team that helps decide our company's 401k investments. I was striving to learn more about this arena when I asked our investment manager advisor if there was a particular book I should read to help me broaden my base of knowledge to help our employees. I hoped there was an *Investment Advice for Dummies Who Serve on 401k Committees* or something like this! Instead, our advisor recommended I go to *FiduciaryNews.com*. He told me Chris' writings would help me the most. I'm grateful for his guidance and the knowledge I am amassing!"
> ➤ Mark Liston, CFE, President, Glass Doctor, Waco, Texas

"Most individual investors think of managing their 401k account as an unpleasant but necessary task. Chris Carosa flips that thinking, and with his offbeat wit, shows how your 401k plan can be an engaging opportunity to take control of your retirement. *Hey! What's My Number?* will zap your investing apathy and jump start your retirement planning – regardless of your age or investing experience."

> Greg Carpenter, CEO, Employee Fiduciary, LLC, Mobile, Alabama

"As baby boomers move like lemmings to the retirement cliff, Carosa uses his real-time experience to offer practical advice, suggestions and whimsical encouragement for maximizing the financial aspects of retirement to both the individual lemming, as well as the herd. This stuff ("how much money will I need?") can be both intimidating as well as disturbing, but by following Carosa's guidance (and hopefully, beginning as early as possible – before the retirement cliff is in sight) – some decent peace of mind and relaxation may be obtainable."

> Dick Clarke, CPCU, CIC, RPLU, Insurance Consultant, Author, Expert Witness and Teacher, Atlanta, Georgia

"Carosa has a way of breaking through to readers, debunking myths, and creating simple to understand analogies for difficult subject matter unlike any other author in the financial world. *Hey! What's My Number* is a valuable resource for everyone from novice 401k plan participants to expert financial professionals."

> Adrian A. Disantagnese, President and Founder, iPay Solutions and iPlan Retirement, Rochester, New York

"Chris has a knack for talking about the complexities of investing and retirement planning in an easy to understand and entertaining fashion. This book has something for both the 401k participant as well as the plan sponsor/fiduciary and should be required reading, especially for those who are either just starting their career and retirement planning as well as those who have put off facing the retirement planning challenge for too long. The book takes a different and captivating approach to retirement planning that will make the topic less intimidating. The concepts are very intriguing and the challenging of MPT and traditional asset allocation thinking is very thought provoking."

> Darren Rieger, Director of Benefits, Itron, Liberty Lake, Washington

For my children: Cesidia, Catarina, and Peter. They, together with their mother, have made my lifetime dream come true. I hope they'll soon take to heart what I've written here and implement it so they'll never have to worry about living a comfortable retirement.

TABLE OF CONTENTS

Section One: Overview

Section Two: Just the Facts

Section Three: False Roads

Section Four: The Power of You

Section Five: Your Personal Plan

Section Six: Appendices

FOREWORD

Today's 401k enrollment meeting process is a farce. There's simply too much to learn, with too little time. There's a "one size fits all" mentality that ignores the obvious (age, salary, income replacement, etc.).

For 25 years I've had ring-side seats in various employers' 401k enrollment meetings. in I've watched employees struggle to digest complicated financial concepts and hear about the 100 year history of the financial markets compressed into a convenient 15 minute camp-fire chat. I feel, like many in the audience, that I've been transported to a distant land, forced to learn a foreign language. Terms like "dollar cost averaging" and "asset allocation diversification" are not part of any normal conversation you'll hear at your local grocery market or coffee shop. As expected, many in the audience withdraw in their seats, with head scratching and glazed-over stares, and many are left wondering "when will this end so I can get back to work?"

This scene unfolds every day at companies that sponsor 401k plans offering employee's a choice on how their money is invested. It's unrealistic to expect any employee, no matter how educated or high (or low) their level of enthusiasm for the subject matter, to make a prudent decision on what steps to take to achieve a successful retirement. To do it right requires an effort and expertise that can't be reduced into a pre-packaged 25 minute presentation or a silver-bullet investment product containing a mix of ingredients promising happy returns with no worry.

Retirement plan sponsors require the help of experts who have a long and proven track-record of success serving as an independent fiduciary (a fancy term meaning "taking care of another person's money"). Some of the better retirement plan fiduciaries understand the difficulty employers face in solving the "what to do" question for their employees. Among these fiduciaries, the "best of the best" are able to simplify the "what to do" equation. They apply their knowledge and experience into a workable solution that's understood and attainable by overburdened plan sponsors. Chris Carosa has shown the way here in his previous book, the widely acclaimed *401(k) Fiduciary Solutions*.

In his latest book — the one you're holding in your hands right now — Chris again solves the "what to do" puzzle, this time for retirement plan participants. In *Hey! What's My Number?* he applies his expertise and years of experience working as an entrusted expert to provide clarity with goal-oriented, targeted results for the typical employee. I've not only read what he's written here, I've seen it work in person. You see, I've watched Chris present the materials contained in this book to live audiences. I've seen their faces transform from the hopeless look of "how can I ever do this?" to smiles of delight that shout "I can't believe it's that easy!"

Chris can habitually do three things the average 401k education meeting presenter fails to consistently achieve. First, he doesn't get hung up in the minutia of investments and market theory. Second, he speaks in a witty conversational tone that reduces complex ideas into easy-to-understand everyday images. (I especially like the muscle car metaphor that runs throughout the book.) Finally, he focuses on the handful of actions that employees have total control over and that can lead them to a comfortable and enjoyable retirement.

In doing these three things, as you'll see in this book, Chris helps those most in need. He simplifies the process so that the "Average Joe/Jane" can benefit, allowing them to achieve better retirement outcomes. Chris takes the complicated procedure of saving and investing for retirement, employs his proven research and long-standing knowledge of behavioral economics, and boils it down to user-friendly mechanics. Couple these mechanics with today's technology (which, in keeping with the automobile metaphor, he calls your "retirement check-engine" light), and you have a powerful weapon for retirement investors of all ages to use in their struggle to meet and even exceed their retirement Goal-Oriented Target.

Chris Carosa has provided a unique approach towards solving a long-standing question of employers who sponsor 401k plans: How can we get our employees to save more? By shifting the primary focus on saving rather than relying solely on picking the right investment products, *Hey! What's My Number?* provides the answer to this question for both retirement plan sponsors and retirement investors. I'm sure you'll smile with delight as you read it — and not just because of the book's often humorous approach!

Richard Burke
Principal – Retirement Plan Consulting & Administration Practice
Burke Group
Rochester, New York

ACKNOWLEDGEMENTS

I must immediately credit Bev Ludke, Human Resources Director for the Brockport Auxiliary Service Corporation at The College of Brockport. Based on the recommendation of one of her colleagues, she called me up out of the blue one day and asked if I could provide a one-hour presentation to her employees on the general subject of 401k investing. From this one exercise on a mild winter day in January 2013 blossomed the book you now hold in your hands. Of course, if you're reading the ebook version it would be the characters on the device in your hand, not the device itself, that have blossomed.

I also want to thank Carol Chowaniec of Springville Manufacturing in Springville, New York who, after having seen a similar presentation, urged me to put it in a form that more people can easily access. (She originally suggested a video to capture the full value of my performance, but I hope she's OK with a book. At least for now.)

The cover represents the combined artistic talents of my daughter Catarina Lena Carosa and my niece and goddaughter Teresa Florence Carosa. I really wanted something that crosses the generations (from millennial through to baby boomers) and they delightfully delivered.

Any book meant for the general public like this one requires sounding boards, reading critics and, well, just about anyone willing to help. I of course must thank the readers of *FiduciaryNews.com* and the many professionals I've interviewed over the years who were willing to offer their thoughts and analysis. I'm especially grateful to my daughter Cesidia Maria Carosa who read what I thought was the final manuscript with the eyes of a twenty-something-year-old and not only asked me to explain such terms as "DOL" and "volatility," but also offered some excellent reformatting suggestions that vastly improved the beginning and end of the book.

While an honest author has to vet his ideas with potential readers, a successful author must unscrew his ego cap and place it at the door as he asks an experienced book editor to go through his final manuscript. Once again I've been lucky to have Mark Frisk do this for me. Mark brings with him the traditional and rare breeding of the New York City literary circles as well as someone who understand me and my little, shall we say, eccentricities.

It goes without saying that every writer needs two things to write well: time and a supportive family. Time is always a limited resource, but the support from my nuclear and extended family goes on to infinity. They are genuinely as pleased as I am every time I convert one of my many manuscripts into a published book.

Finally, I've said this before, I'll say it again, and I'll repeat this in every book I write. None of this would be doable without my wife, Betsy. She is my soul mate. She inspires me to write, reads everything I write, proofs everything I write, and owns the company that publishes everything I write. Without her, I'd be just another guy with a blog. She is Beatrice to my Dante, Dulcenea to my Don Quixote and, especially for her, Cathy to my Heathcliff. (She's a fan of *Wuthering Heights*. I prefer to avoid anything from the Victorian Era. Hey, who said soul mates had to agree on everything?)

Christopher Carosa
Mendon, New York
July 15, 2014

INTRODUCTION:
THE SECRET TO RETIREMENT SUCCESS

I stood in front of 300 employees, both union and non-union, from part-time dining hall workers to veteran executives. The head of HR had brought me in for one purpose: to convince the average twenty-five year old making $25,000 a year to begin saving for retirement. Yet the crowd contained such a mix of people, a mix of backgrounds, and a mix of ages that the circumstances demanded I provide a little something for everyone. Ironically, I knew the likelihood of being rehired depended on how the more practiced professionals viewed my performance, not how well I entertained the constituency I had been engaged to address.

Nonetheless, I remained confident I could titillate all segments of the variegated crowd. Why? I knew the secret of PowerPoint presentations. Don't get me wrong. As an aspiring orator (or stand-up comedian, I haven't quite decided yet), I really dislike the impersonal distraction PowerPoint has become to presentations. Still, I've learned there's a time when it's OK to dare to be a top-rated AM disc jockey (which I was back during the days when AM still played music) and a time to play the role of the droll motivational speaker.

When you want to entertain the masses, you become a shock-jock, always coming at them with something completely different.

When you want senior management to rehire you, you play it safe, always sticking to the tried and true because they expect the expected.

On this particular job, despite the straightforward nature of my marching orders, experience told me that success required I do the impossible. Fortunately, fate had placed me in this position before. In fact, it seems fate has placed me in this same situation a depressingly great number of times. I don't think fate likes me too much.

Which gets us to the secret of PowerPoint presentations. Everyone expects a PowerPoint presentation, but nobody expects the Spanish Inquisition. Yet, the former tends to put people to sleep while the latter almost always leads to a memorable — if not historic — event. The secret, then, is to marry the two. Almost anyone who's seen one of my presentations can tell you it's different. But this book isn't about how to create a successful PowerPoint presentation. It's about how to achieve retirement success.

It's also why I started with the story of this particular presentation. Because, just minutes before I was to appear on stage, I had discovered a bug in my PowerPoint presentation. It wasn't in the computer. It wasn't in the program. It was in the specific presentation I had created for this specific afternoon.

This, dear reader, is a critical lesson to learn as you plan for retirement: Even the best-laid plans are doomed to fail for want of the most miniscule and unexpected reasons. Don't count on being lucky. Count on being unlucky. It's only after you concede to this reality that you can really succeed.

This book doesn't answer the second most asked question everyone wants to know: "How much money do I need to retire?" No, it answers the most important question everyone should want to know: "What's my number?" The number isn't the final total at the end — that's pretty cloudy. What you'll discover by reading this book is that the number is really a simple single-digit (I hope) number that, although it may change over time, is something you have far greater control over than you think.

Life always hits you with unexpected complications. Some of these complications can be fun — like winning tickets to a concert or a sporting event. Some of these complications can be the opposite of fun — like totaling your car in an accident. And some of these complications can be fulfilling — like watching your child's face grin upon achieving some major feat. The point is, you don't necessarily know exactly when these surprises will happen, but there's no question they will. Some you can plan for, some you can't. It doesn't mean they'll prevent you from succeeding. Quite the contrary, as long as you expect the unexpected and have a deliberative process to execute once the unexpected happens, you will succeed.

So, what happened when I discovered the bug in my PowerPoint presentation?

I went on with the show. Because, you see, the secret of PowerPoint presentations isn't what appears on the screen, it's the person performing the presentation. In front of those 300 people, success did not depend on pretty graphs, font size or cute animations. It depended on only one thing…

…me.

Like your retirement, success depends on only one thing…

…you.

SECTION ONE:

– OVERVIEW –

HOW TO BEST USE THIS TOOL

CHAPTER ONE:
THE PURPOSE AND NATURE OF THIS BOOK

When I sat down to write *Hey! What's My Number?* I did so with the thought of helping as many people as possible. You see, I've learned a lot in the three decades-plus I've been in the investment and retirement plan business. I've learned even more as a writer and journalist on the subject.

By my late twenties, I had absorbed enough about planning for retirement that I decided I could begin the first phase of my retirement when I was 45 years old. I say "first phase" because as a kid I noticed a common fact about retirement that really turned me off. Too often, people would die soon after they retired. I did not consider this a good thing. For this reason, I decided my retirement would consist of several phases. In all but the final stage, I would continue working. Through each stage, though, the effort required the "work" would diminish.

I guess at this point I had better define what I mean by "work" and what I mean by "retirement." Work means doing something you get paid for. Retirement means living a relaxing, fulfilling, and happy lifestyle. For many, retirement begins when work ends. For some, like me, the terms "work" and "retirement" are not mutually exclusive.

Want an example?

Think Paul Newman. Here's a famous actor who worked until the day he died. Like most successful older actors, he worked when he wanted to, not because he had to. He also didn't just rely on his physical performances as a way to earn money. He established a side business to sell his "Newman's Own" food products. Throughout it all, he continued being a celebrity. Did he ever "retire"? For those who think of retirement as spending the last years of your life watching *M*A*S*H* reruns in a Florida condo, Paul Newman never retired. For those like me, we look at Paul Newman and we say, "Hey! That's how I want to retire!"

The purpose of this book isn't to show you how to retire like Paul Newman did (I'll save that story for another book).

No. The idea of this book came from presentations like the one I discussed in the Introduction — and from every article I've written, book I've authored, video I've produced, and whatever type of media

I've ever appeared in. I want to share the lessons of accomplishment I've learned from successful retirees with as many people as imaginable. I figured there's no way possible every potential retiree could see me live and in person, so I decided to write an easy-to-read book. The actual title of this book, however, did come from the presentation mentioned in the Introduction. Upon completing my prepared remarks, I asked the audience if they had any thoughts, questions, or inanely funny stories they wished to share. The very first query a member of the audience shouted out was "Hey! What's my number?"

The phrase "What's my number?" has become popular in a series of commercials (current as of this writing) for a certain financial services company. The ads refer to the total dollar value one needs to retire. While the campaign correctly implies everyone has his or her own unique number, by selecting the total dollar value, it failed in two ways. First, the actual precision of the numbers (down to the very dollar) implies a false sense of credibility. As real financial professionals know (as opposed to those creative ad men responsible for the memorable commercial), the total value needed to secure a comfortable retirement constantly changes, even during retirement. Furthermore, given the range of error, it's not really practical to present the total dollar value down to a single digit's place.

Far more important, though, is the sense of the magnitude of the number. When I speak to individual employees, I find that telling them they need to accumulate a number with seven digits (that means it's in the millions) often intimidates them. Sure, they need to know what that number is, and there's plenty of ways to calculate that number. But if I, like the financial service company's famous advertisement, stopped with that number, too many retirement investors would leave the meeting depressed. People, on average, have little experience that allows them to readily visualize how they can personally attain such a large number. Worse, politicians and the mass media make seven-digit numbers sound like something only found in the top 1% of the population. (Those who know otherwise have probably read *The Millionaire Next Door: The Surprising Secrets of America's Wealthy*, by Thomas J. Stanley and William D. Danko.) A surprisingly large number of "regular" (i.e., not top 1%) people are either now or on their way to becoming millionaires — and many if not most have their company's 401k plan to thank for it.

Still, the idea of attaining a seven-digit number, especially for younger workers, seems downright inconceivable. Financial professionals need to recognize this. Many have already adjusted their "talk" to avoid such de-motivating factors.

Here's how I do it.

First, and you'll see this specific example in Chapter 21, I show them how a 15 year-old can become a near-millionaire merely by saving a thousand dollars a year for sixteen years. You should see the eyes of the audience pop open when I show them how incredibly easy this is. In fact, many middle-aged folks — no doubt ones with teenage children — come up to me after my presentation and ask if I can package that one slide for them in a way to show their children. (I'm working on that). What's more, lately I've been amazing crowds (including professionals) by showing them how newborns can become multi-millionaires when they retire by just investing $1,000 a year through high school graduation. (No joke. You can read about the idea in Appendix V. I call it the "Child IRA." It doesn't exist yet, but smart people like author and radio talk-show host Ric Edelman have figured out a way to come close to duplicating it. Hopefully Congress can make a real "Child IRA.")

The second thing I do, after showing them the big honkin' seven-digit number, is get them to focus on a different number. This number is much smaller. It's much easier to digest. It's much easier to understand. And, especially for the young, it reveals just how easy it is for them to become millionaires and retire in that comfortable lifestyle they can only dream of.

That's the purpose of this book: To help you retire in the way that you want.

In summary:

Here's what not to expect: *Hey! What's My Number?* is not an enchanted elixir that will magically transport you from your current life to the life of Riley. It will not give you the "secret numbers" that will allow you to win any one of life's many lotteries. It won't present a foolproof method guaranteed to work 100% of the time (remember the "Nobody Expects the Spanish Inquisition" Rule in the Introduction). Finally, I promise not to bore you with treatise upon treatise of investment philosophy. In fact — and your investment adviser might be afraid to admit this to you — you'll be surprised to discover just how unimportant investments are in the grand scheme of things. That being said, there is one common investment mistake so many retirement investors make that Congress passed a law to discourage —

but not prevent — it. I'll tell you what it is later on in this book. In the meantime, what's the best way to prevent it? Either maintain a rigorous self-discipline or work with a trusted investment adviser. Whichever way you pick is fine by me. Just make sure to pick one and buy my book. If you or any other reader chooses to employ the services of investment advisers, make sure they buy this book, too. Indeed, it is with unabashed self-promotion that I would encourage you to encourage investment advisers to buy this book for each of their clients. (I priced it low enough for them to do that.)

Here's what to expect: I'll explore each of the four critical steps you need to know and execute in order to live a successful retirement. In the chapters covering these steps, I'll introduce you to some pretty sophisticated academic theory, but don't let that scare you. I wouldn't be sharing it with you if I didn't think you could understand it. Indeed, I bet, after you read about the particular research studies I mention, your reaction will be, "I already knew that." In the end, I won't show you what your big seven-digit number is, instead I'll show you what your real number is, what it means, and how you can use that information to help give you a better chance to retire in comfort.

But before we can get there, we need to bring everyone up to speed. Everything in this book is about you, and only you. I'll show you how easy it is to get what you need to live a comfortable retirement. I'll share with you, through the words of dozens of retirement planning professionals, the success stories — stories that you can easily duplicate — that have enabled people to achieve their lifetime dream. Only you, however, can make sure everything that needs to get done gets done. Yes, you might ask (and it probably is a good idea to) an investment adviser for help, but, ultimately, it comes down to your own self-discipline. If you want to achieve your lifetime dream, it's important you have a method to help you, but it's more critical for you to knuckle down and actually do the tasks.

Finally, as you trod along your journey to retirement, each step might appear insignificant. Rest assured, making a commitment to put one foot forward starts you on a process that will have wonderful results.

So, without further ado, and I don't mean to understate their significance, let's start this journey with the…

CHAPTER TWO:
4 STEPS THAT WILL CHANGE YOUR LIFE

You can accomplish almost anything, even the impossible. I bet you never thought you were all-powerful. In fact, if you're like most people, you don't. And that's OK. Not everyone can invent a cure for polio, create the assembly line method of manufacturing, or discover a way to reduce integrated circuits to the size of a fingernail. Really. It's OK. We can get by with only a handful of people who believe they can accomplish the undoable. We'll leave it to those folks to find a way to prevent cancer, to uncover a way to reduce energy costs, and to invent a practical anti-gravity device.

You don't have to do any of those things.

What you do have to do is the one thing only you can do something about: prepare yourself to retire comfortably. Now, I know what you're thinking. You're thinking, "Haven't I read where it's impossible for the average person to retire?" "Haven't I heard politicians speak of the coming retirement crisis?" "Haven't I seen documentaries explaining why America's private retirement system is nothing but a huge gamble?"

That's right. You have read, heard, and seen all these things. And there are people today — and will be in the future — who should be retired but aren't. When it comes to living a comfortable retirement, just because some people fail does not mean you must follow their lead. In fact, I can tell you there's a better group of people to follow: those who have successfully navigated the savings waters and are now comfortably relaxing on the beach of retirement.

I can tell you this because I know these people. Many of them are not rocket scientists (although a few are). Most of them held regular jobs — whether skilled or unskilled, hourly or salaried, professional or non-professional. That so many people from so many different backgrounds are living a comfortable retirement should tell you the same thing I discovered long ago: The path to an easy post-career retreat is as well-trodden as it is well-defined. You only need a road map to lead you there — and the discipline to continue the trip once you've started.

Taking this journey requires no advanced degree, no advanced deposits, indeed no sums of money far beyond what you're used to seeing on a day-to-day basis. Furthermore, walking along these steps does not demand any special abilities at all. You just have to want to do it. Of course, by "want to do it," I'm talking about the old "actions speak louder than words" thing. You can read about these steps over and over, but unless and until you start acting on them, you'll never get off of square one.

We all dream of a cozy retirement nestled close to the ones we love in an idyllic peaceful setting. Many would call this "success." Success begins with but a single step onto the path. Now, here's the amazing truth. The path has already been laid out. You don't have to hack your way through an unchartered jungle to find retirement success. Others have blazed the trail before you. You need only learn their route and commit yourself to the voyage, just like you would for any other goal you wish to undertake.

Julia Chung, Practice Leader for Wealth Strategies Facet Advisors in British Columbia, Canada, says, "Just like when we are creating a career path (School, Internship, Junior Staff, Senior Staff, Management and so forth), there is a path to retirement success. The lottery isn't going to provide the vast majority of us with a windfall. The reality is that careful planning and management of those factors that you can actually control — regardless of how boring they really are — makes the difference between success and failure."

The path to retirement success is surprisingly short. It only contains four steps. What are these four steps? Why are they so important? And, how do we know they are the four steps that will change your life? I've divided *Hey! What's My Number?* into sections, each of which digs deeper into these questions. If you're in a hurry or think you already know everything you need to know about saving for retirement, feel free to go directly to Section Five. That section outlines how to use the free on-line *Hey! What's My Number?* Retirement Readiness Calculator to construct, modify, and monitor your own personal retirement readiness plan.

Of course, if you are the kind of person who is in a hurry or who thinks they already know everything they need to know about saving for retirement, you're the exact kind of person who MUST read Sections Two, Three, and Four. Remember, nobody expects the Spanish Inquisition. You never know what you don't know.

While the remaining sections of this book discuss the four steps in the kind of detail you'll need in order to get started, I'll satisfy your immediate curiosity by briefly describing them here.

Step #1: Understand the Basics of Retirement Success. Before you can bake a cake, you need to embrace the fundamentals of kitchen physics. You know what I mean: How to measure ingredients; How to know which pots, pans, and mixing bowls to use; and, How to best employ the variety of kitchen appliances at your disposal. Failure to understand even the most basic things about cooking might lead to a cake that collapses, a foul tasting dessert, or even a hand burned by touching a hot oven rack. The same is true about "baking" a triumphant retirement. To succeed, you need to grasp the basics of savings and investments. This involves a little bit of math, but, thank goodness, it's the simple stuff from elementary school, not that calculus mess from high school. Understanding the basics of savings and investments will begin to teach you both what is within reason and the importance of commitment when it comes to your retirement. Each of these often represent the difference between success and failure.

Some, like Steve Garfink, Founder of Retire Now or Later in San Jose, California, rely on Social Security, and for older folks, this may be an appropriate strategy. Garfink tells me that "each annual cohort of retirees leaves nearly $50 billion on the table in benefits they would otherwise have collected over their lifetimes with a better strategy." He feels that the "single most important element in determining retirement financial success is getting your Social Security claiming strategy right." Furthermore, he warns, "People fail to plan a strategy because most don't even understand that there is anything to plan."

For many, though, especially among those younger than age 50, there is a waning confidence in Social Security. "Most would agree that Social Security will be worth less going forward," says Howard Safer, Chief Executive Officer of Argent Money in Nashville, Tennessee. He says, "The antidote is saving and investing not just for a 'rainy day,' but for a hurricane."

Step #2: Avoid the Common Mistakes of Retirement Savers. It helps to know the right things to do, but many times it's vastly more important to know what not to do. Fortunately for today's savers, we have generations of other retirement savers' experience to show us what to avoid. Unfortunately for those older savers, we've only recently begun to understand how to explain these common errors. Most of them fall under the definition of behavioral economics, a relatively new science that for a long time had been shunned in the academic community. Today, the field is not only accepted (its founders were awarded a Nobel Prize), but it might even be considered ascendant. Why? Because people are not perfect (i.e., not rational) and the best way to improve is to admit to those imperfections. We've come a long way since the academic-industrial complex introduced the world to the techno-jargon that has done more to frighten individual savers than anything else. Behavioral economics speaks in the language of common sense, something the typical investor appreciates a lot more than the arcane stochastic formulae of earlier investment theories.

Jeff S. Vollmer, Managing Partner at Hyde Park Wealth Management in Cincinnati/Columbus, Ohio, believes these common errors "should be avoided at all costs." They can have a long-lasting impact. Vollmer says "mistakes can actually set retirees back in terms of the progress they make towards longer term objectives. Once made, small mistakes can set one's portfolio back. Larger mistakes can actually adversely impact one's quality of living."

"Avoiding common mistakes is a macro concept in that it impacts everything," says Michael T. Prus, President of Scale Investment Group, LLC in White Lake and Grand Blanc, Michigan. "Macro" means "the big picture." This represents the fundamental savings strategy. Its impact can far exceed (for better or worse) the impact of tactical choices like investments. In other words, no matter how well your investment picks perform, you will find you won't achieve your retirement goal if you made a big mistake in your savings strategy. Prus says, "Making significant errors here [your savings strategy] and having the right investments is still unlikely to provide the desired results. Only after the macro issues are under control should micro issues like specific fund selection be considered."

Step #3: Emphasize the Three Critical Components to Retirement Success. Since we've just mentioned "specific fund selection," allow me to remind you of the findings of a 2012 Wharton study. The paper identified the four components that lead to retirement success. Of the four, the investor controls three: When to start saving; How much to save; and, When to retire. The fourth — investment return — has traditionally been the focus of retirement plans (often at

Small boats sink large ships ^.

the expense of encouraging savings). Yet, oddly enough, the Wharton study calculated that the real-life difference between the optimal investment selection versus the average investment selection could be made up simply by working four more months before retiring. Who'da thunk it? But it just goes to show, we ought to be talking about savings, not investments.

Prus says, "Investors all too often focus on return when they discuss saving for retirement. Returns are largely, if not entirely, out of our control as market participants. Even an investor who has great returns may fail to save enough for retirement if they don't set aside enough to begin with."

"Investors who spend too much time worrying about the incremental outperformance of individual positions are often chasing their tails," says Vollmer, who continues, "Each of the first three components are more or less meant to help one leverage the time-value of money, as well as the time until retirement. They can be proactively controlled and managed, and so should be begun as soon as possible. The last factor is a product of the marketplace, which is completely out of the investor's hands. Every investor will have multiple market cycles during which his money is invested and working on his behalf. Maximize the first three factors and the fourth becomes much less important over time."

Step #4: Create, Implement, and Monitor a Personal Plan. In the long run, this is the one step that truly matters (and the one you should complete first). After all, the best way to get where you want to be is to make a plan to get there. Some people have no problem making plans for themselves. However, common sense tells me, (and you, too), what plenty of studies show to be true: compared to those who don't, retirement savers who use a professional adviser tend to increase their chances of reaching their goals. The reason can be as simple as professionals having a greater awareness of typical savers' errors (see Step #2); thus, they can better help their clients avoid those errors. Additionally, an adviser or "coach" frequently possesses the advantage of objectivity and the broad view to understand that cookie-cutter solutions usually don't work. (This may be why, like internet-based "free" medical advice before them, web-based "robo" advisers are doomed to fail.) Professional advisers (the human kind) add tremendous value by forcing clients to consider their own personal situations and needs. No one is ever truly average. Each investor has unique wants, desires, and, ultimately, goals. Some folks can focus on their individual plan just fine by themselves, while others might require an objective third party for help. And by "objective third party," I mean a real person, not a machine. (Did I make that point enough times?)

"Online calculators are a great start, but they are only a start," says Prus. "They largely fail to consider your standard of living during retirement. These factors, as well as unforeseen expenses, can take a large bite out of retirement savings if they are not carefully considered by the individual on a case-by-case basis, not through a generic calculator." He didn't say anything about the "Spanish Inquisition," but, if you're paying attention to what you're reading, you know that's what he's talking about.

Vollmer says, "We know that the qualitative side of one's life, through which we make risk management, asset protection, and estate planning decisions, cannot be calculated by a calculator. Only by personalizing these, and weighing these factors against one's quantitative reality, can one begin to truly arrive at sound, long-term financial planning decisions."

Chung provides a fitting conclusion when she says, "Regardless of how normal or boring a person thinks his lifestyle is, everyone is unique. Everyone is different and there is no single solution or calculator — or dollar figure — that will solve the problem for everyone. If it was easy, it wouldn't be a profession. Retirement and financial planning can only ever be a customized individual process, because every single life path is different."

*   *   *   *   *

This represents but a quick overview of the four fundamental steps everyone can take to live a successful retirement. Of course, there are a lot of details in each of these steps. We'll visit those details in the next four sections of this book.

We begin with some basics. How many of the seven simple savings secrets do you know? Find out in the next chapter.

SECTION TWO:

– JUST THE FACTS –

THE BASICS OF RETIREMENT SUCCESS

CHAPTER THREE:
7 SIMPLE SAVING SECRETS EVERY 401K SAVER SHOULD KNOW

I have gone through thousands of retirement analyses over the years. When I was younger, looking mostly at younger people, what I saw scared me. Retirement, that great nebulous beyond, seemed almost a fantasy land. It lay at a distance further than the horizon, unseen, unknown, and unimaginable. Consequently, saving for it appeared to most — including me — like lifting a large twenty-ton boulder. Back in those days, this "saving for a retirement" idea was an obstacle far too enormous for a mere mortal to tackle.

At least not then. Not (for me and many other baby boomers) in the 1980's. Not during the period of the vanishing (and now mostly extinct) pension plan. No, our parents had it easy — they had the best of both worlds. They had the guarantee of a fixed pension and they had the lavish promise of private retirement accounts. What I saw before me was Mount Everest compared to their Pike's Peak. The older generation could merely latch on to the vehicle of their company's retirement fund and drive to the summit of retirement success. The younger generation faced sheer cliffs that required an individual, seemingly superhuman, effort to surmount.

Again, the pure size of the mission dwarfed the confidence of the average twenty-something year old.

Yet, despite the onus of this burden, we heard repeatedly this mantra from our experienced elders: "Every great journey begins with but a single step." In addition to this philosophical tidbit, we had a guidebook of a handful of simple savings secrets. They were so simple they defied belief. Indeed, some young skeptics, too cool to bind themselves to someone else's ideas, opted instead to live as if the world would end tomorrow. For a "lucky" few in that group, it did. For the others in that coterie, they soon learned the price of their hedonism.

But for the rest of us, those willing to take these single steps, we now find ourselves nearing the end of a rainbow. It's remarkable. We were told our entire life this rainbow could never exist. And yet it does. Within our very real grasp sits a pot of gold, the fruits of our life's labors, the milk to our retirement shake, the one thing that guarantees us comfort in our remaining years. And, to think, it all started with that fistful of simple savings secrets we almost tossed aside.

What are these simple savings secrets? Why do they work? And, how can you take advantage of them? We each have our own shorthand for these secrets. How we refer to them depends on our upbringing, our education, and, to some extent, our own personal values. As Chief Contributing Editor at *FiduciaryNews.com*, I've had the honor to speak with hundreds of financial professionals from all across America. This has given me a chance to taste the different flavors of this same sauce of success. No matter what spices the cook uses, the cuisine pleases the palate, which in this case, really means the wallet.

So, let the trumpets blare and the drums pound. Here are the seven most important simple savings secrets every 401k saver should know.

#1: <u>Make a Commitment.</u> The best way to commit yourself is by stating a specific goal and then coming up with a plan to attain that goal. Mitchell D. Weiss has taught as an adjunct in the Economics & Finance Department at the University of Hartford's Barney School of Business in West Hartford, Connecticut. He believes it's important to "start by establishing the objective of the money (in this case, retirement)." The plan need not be elaborate; it can be as modest as "saving." The point isn't the precision, it's simply the fact that it's easier to plan for an event (like retirement) if you start earlier. Elle Kaplan, CEO & Founding Partner at Lexion Capital Management LLC in New York City, says, "Planning for retirement should begin decades before you plan to retire."

#2: <u>Spend Less Than You Earn.</u> It seems so obvious, yet this savings secret often evaporates once one graduates from school. As a student, money is tight and — not counting student loans — cash flow represents a very real issue. Financial discipline isn't just second nature, it's the law of the land. After all, you can't spend it if you don't have it. Once schools unleash their graduates, the pent up demand spews out. Give a young graduate a credit card and see what happens. Ilene Davis is a financial planner at Financial Independence Services in Cocoa, Florida. For her, the most critical simple savings secret is "spend less than you earn and invest the difference." Tim Shanahan, President and Chief Investment Strategist at Compass Capital Corporation in Braintree, Massachusetts, agrees with this simple savings secret. He tells his clients to "live on less than your means allow."

#3: Pay Yourself First. Here's another deceptively simple savings secret. We often have to prioritize, and too often we sacrifice our own needs for the needs of others. When it comes to saving for retirement, not only is it OK to be selfish, but your very survival may depend on it. Remember, you're alone on that sheer cliff. You can't count on anyone else. It's solely your responsibility. Do yourself a favor. Pay yourself first. Karen Lee, owner of Karen Lee and Associates, LLC in Atlanta, Georgia, has been a financial planner for 25 years. She's spent most of that time helping people save for retirement. She advises her clients to "save first over all other purchases, as if it was a bill you owed." Shanahan says, "Pay yourself first. Make room in your budget to save for retirement before the discretionary spending." Elle Kaplan tries to help clients avoid getting tripped up by this simple savings secret. She warns, "Focusing on budgeting and penny-pinching is not the way to think about saving. Think of it as paying your future self. You can't afford not to. Paying yourself should be an automatic first priority, just like any other bill."

#4: Start Early. It's funny. Many young savers get tripped up worrying too much about investment choices rather than simply starting to save. (This so-called "paradox of choice" occurs when too many choices cause people to delay decisions.) In reality, it's better to just start saving with no undo emphasis on investing. "It's about time, not timing," says Davis. In other words, time heals all poor investment decisions, so the earlier you start saving, the less critical investment performance will become. Lee says, "Save young." She points out "the money you save in your 20's and 30's is your most valuable savings in your 60's." Eric Heckman, President of Worry Less Wealth in San Jose, California, says, "Start now. Something — anything." Elle Kaplan says, "Make it easy and automatic: set up a regular transfer to occur as soon as your paycheck hits your account that deposits the money directly into your investment account." (This might be needed for some IRA-based retirement plans, but the company sponsor of a 401k plan should automatically make this direct deposit from your salary upon issuing every paycheck.)

#5: Save Money By Using Tax-Deferred Savings Vehicles. Almost everyone has heard of the 401k or the IRA. The government allows you to skip out of paying income taxes for any contribution you place in these vehicles. Of course, you'll still have to pay taxes when you finally take the money out of these accounts, but, ideally, you'll be in a lower tax bracket then. More importantly, you can actually increase your net take home pay (including the amount you save in these tax deferred accounts) by saving in retirement plans. Tara L. Mashack-Behney, Director of Investment Consulting at Conrad Siegel Investment Advisors, Inc. in Harrisburg, Pennsylvania, explains why this is so. "Federal income taxes are not withheld from regular 401k contributions," she says. "So for example, a $100 contribution may only cost you $85 in take-home pay. (However, your actual deduction may be more or less depending on your income tax bracket, number of withholding allowances, etc.)."

#6: Always Grab the Free Money. When a company offers to match any contribution you make, take full advantage of that match. Shanahan combines an earlier savings secret with this one when he says, "Save early — as soon as you have a job — and take full advantage of employer matching." Rachele Bouchand, Director of Financial Planning at Clark Nuber, P.S. in Bellevue, Washington, says, "Take advantage of employer matching in retirement accounts. Don't leave money on the table."

#7: Now Save More. There's always a way to save a little more. Lee puts it succinctly: "Save a lot." Heckman adds a little more color when he says, "If your plan has an auto-escalating feature, use it. If not, put a note to increase every year." Elle Kaplan is downright specific. She says, "Everyone should aim to save a minimum of 20% of every paycheck." Bouchand has a very insightful way to explain the advantages of saving more. She says it "benefits you two ways: you have money you can use in the future and it forces you to live on a lower standard of living now. It's hard to decrease your standard of living in retirement if you're used to a higher one in your working years."

It's remarkable what following these seven simple savings secrets can lead to. Now that I'm older, I can see firsthand how abiding by this sage advice has helped not only me, but also many others like me. It's amazing, but true.

And to think, it all started with one small step. Ironically, this "savings" device called the 401k has proven more reliable than the traditional pension plan. By the late 1980s, corporate pensions became an albatross too burdensome to carry. In the worst cases, they became mere assets in the corporate takeover game. Whatever the reason, they've mostly disappeared from the private sector. Although some workers found themselves receiving fewer retirement benefits than promised, most older private pensioners continue to get their monthly checks. Fewer of today's employees in the private sector will ever see money coming from a pension plan.

The same, unfortunately, cannot be said of public employee pensions. That's a tug-of-war that's going on even as this book is being written. While the private pension arena exposed certain other problems with the defined benefit model, it has been the public pensions that have revealed the true Ponzi nature of pension plans in general. Without sustained growth in both population and the economy — the fuel that feeds the beast of the pension — these funds will run out of money before all the retirees have been paid. Such is the fate of all Ponzi schemes. Only, this one is legal (at least at the time of writing).

In the end, those who entered the workforce in the 1980's and who chose the road less taken (i.e., the 401k retirement savings vehicle) find themselves in a much better, much more secure, and much more controllable situation than those who ventured down the path of the pension plan. I repeat: It all started with one small step.

If you're still not convinced you need to start saving right now, I'll let Stanley H. Molotsky, President & CEO at SHM Financial in Philadelphia, Pennsylvania have the last word. "You have to do it and do it now," says Molotsky. "You might want to wait for government programs to help," he adds, "but government programs may not be there in the future, so you have to do it yourself."

Of course, as I said before, there are things you shouldn't do. We'll explore these in the next chapter.

CHAPTER FOUR:
THE TEN "DON'T"S OF 401K SAVINGS

Ever hear the phrase "winning by not losing"? It's one of those classic sports adages that works in everyday life, too. Actually, come to think of it, it probably works more in everyday life than it works in sports. Anyone who's watched their favorite team lose in the final minutes of the game only because their team switched to a "prevent" defense knows what I mean.

(If you don't know, a "prevent" defense is a strategy employed by a team ahead in points — the "prevent" team —that wishes to "win by not losing." Its objective is to "prevent" the other team from scoring on a big play. Ironically, it often yields the result of preventing the "prevent" team from winning since this defensive strategy tends to allow the opponent to score through a series of small plays; thus, eating up valuable time on the clock giving the "prevent" team no chance to score again.)

(Whew! That was a mouthful!)

In real life, though, "winning by not losing" has become the preferred game plan. For example, if you've ever taken a defensive driving course, then you've learned one practical way to employ a "winning by not losing" strategy. Several other good examples come from the financial world. Not only is "winning by not losing" a great formula for budgeting (by building in a contingency for those unexpected costs that always find a way or popping up), it's also helpful when it comes to purchasing (by buying the highest quality, not lowest cost) and investing (by not taking too much risk as a result of "swinging for the fences").

Ah, "Don't swing for the fences." If there's ever been a favorite phrase for speaking the language of "winning by not losing," it must be this baseball cliché. As we all know (and if we don't, we should), trying to hit a home run (i.e., "swinging for the fences") leads to more strike outs than merely trying to hit singles. Rod Carew's late career contract negotiations and the movie *The Natural* aside, many more baseball games are won by big innings where the bases are constantly loaded than by bases-empty home runs. And the best way to get the bases constantly loaded is by hitting singles, i.e., by not "swinging for the fences," i.e., "winning by not losing."

Ah, baseball.

Ah, springtime.

Each spring ushers in not only a new baseball season, but that time of year when many families celebrate significant religious holidays with feasts, ceremonies, and the traditional family gathering around the picture tube to watch a Charlton Heston classic or two (you know the ones I mean, *The Ten Commandments*, *Ben Hur*, *Planet of the Apes*...well, maybe not that last one). Anyway, this leads one to think, what would Moses do today if he were around? No doubt his actions would differ from the agrarian society of ancient Egypt to the post-industrial corporate world of today. Would he be known as a turn-around specialist, parting the sea of red ink to take companies to the Promised Land? Or imagine, if you will, Charlton Heston as the embattled HR manager, frustrated in trying to convince his people to take charge of their lives and save for retirement. He would go, alone, to the penthouse suite and meet with the Man Upstairs who would surely have the wisdom to provide the perfect preventative advice to retirement savers. Perhaps Moses would have then descended from this Mount Sinai with the following Decalogue written on his tablet computer:

#1: Don't Wait to Start. This goes along the line of "Don't put off to tomorrow what you can do today." Brooks Herman, Head of Research at BrightScope in San Diego, California, says, "New savers usually think they can save more later in life when they earn more money. They should start now! Saving money is like exercise: it's a behavioral habit people should start early and do often." Not only is it harder to develop good savings habits when you're older, but waiting causes you to miss all the wonderful delights that come from compounding.

#2: Don't Assume Everything Will be Perfect. If you've forgotten the "Nobody Expects the Spanish Inquisition" Rule, here it is again. Along the way to retirement, you'll need to make several assumptions. You'll even have to repeatedly update those assumptions. It's always safer to err on the side of caution. Elle Kaplan says, "Every assumption you make should be extremely conservative. Your savings becomes your paycheck and must last the rest of your life. It's easy to find ways to spend extra money, but much more difficult to deal with a shortfall."

#3: Don't Fail to Plan. To repeat another ubiquitous phrase here in *Hey! What's My Number?*: "Retirement is a journey that begins with a single step." Such is the planning process. Jeff Stoffer, Principal at Stoffer Wealth Advisers in San Rafael, California, says, "Planning is about answering the questions, 'When can I retire?' and 'Will I have enough money to last my lifetime?' Planning starts with generating ideas about what you need and want in retirement. Visualizing what retirement looks like for you is a step in planning that tends to be overlooked. Planning for the future can seem abstract, almost like fantasizing. In order for us to get excited about it and hold it as a goal, it needs to be attractive to us. We will be more likely to put our money toward it if it is something real in our mind's eye." Which means ... wait for it ... here it comes ... "Those who fail to plan, plan to fail."

#4: Don't Put Off Saving If Your Company Doesn't Match. Worse than not taking the "free" money of company matching is the act of not saving just because the company doesn't match. Stephen D. Iaconis, a financial planner at Bridgeworth Financial, LLC in Birmingham, Alabama says, "A common misconception is that 'if my employer doesn't match, I shouldn't contribute.' This is very dangerous. The only person responsible for your retirement future is you. Save no matter what your employer is matching."

#5: Don't Just Keep Contributing the Same Amount Every Year. Once you start to save, that's great, but it's only the first step. Your contribution percentages should increase as your pay increases. "Commit to increasing each year, give yourself a retirement raise annually," says Paula Hendrickson, Director Retirement Plan Consulting at First Western Trust in the Greater Denver area. She continues, "The sooner you can be contributing between 10-15% the better chance at success. I have never met a participant in a retirement plan who told me 'I saved too much'."

#6: Don't Assume You'll Need Less Money When You Retire. Joseph F. Ready, Executive Vice President at Wells Fargo Institutional Retirement and Trust in Charlotte, NC believes too many people incorrectly say to themselves "I will need a lot less money in retirement than I do now." He says, "Many experts recommend that people should expect to spend about 80% of their annual pre-retirement household income during retirement. That may seem high, but the retirement landscape is changing, as baby boomers prepare for more active retirements than earlier generations. Hobby-related expenses, travel, entertainment, home repairs/remodeling, health care, and other costs can all boost the price tag of an active retirement."

#7: Don't Assume You Won't Live Long. Ready also believes people convince themselves, "I won't live that long." This is a problem, he notes. "The good news is that Americans are living longer," he says. He adds, "But with a longer life expectancy comes the need to fund a longer retirement. Building a nest egg to sustain 30 years of retirement (instead of 10 to 15 years) can help ensure that you don't outlive your savings."

#8: Don't Bring a Knife to a Gun Fight. Michelle Ford, CEO of LifeLong Retirement Corp in Bridgewater, New Jersey, says, "Understand there are two parts to retirement planning. There is the accumulation (build the pot) phase and then the distribution (spend down) phase. If you understand that there will be a spend-down then the accumulation phase should be planned with this in mind. In other words, don't just build the assets, put them in the right tax advantaged accounts (in line with 'don't bring a knife to a gun fight'). The distribution phase is all about income planning so educate yourself on: A) How much you actually spend; B) Your guaranteed income sources and their applicable rules/choices; and, C) How do taxes impact your varied sources of income and how do they interlace together."

#9: Don't Leave Your Retirement Savings in the Company's Plan When You Retire. There's a lot of confusion on this one. Some talking heads say not to rollover into an IRA because there are better fiduciary protections in the company plan. This will remain true until the regulators place IRAs under fiduciary protection. They also say staying in the company plan is cheaper. Sometimes this is true, but it's not always the case. Many, however, advise to rollover because it allows more freedom (but at the price of *caveat emptor*, at least until regulators place IRAs under the aforementioned fiduciary protection). They also cite the advantage of ready access to your funds (always true once you rollover, but still sometimes true if you leave the money in the plan). Stephanie Ackler, CFA, Managing Director of Investments at Ackler Wealth Management of Wells Fargo Advisors, LLC in New York City says, "When you leave a job or retire, consider rolling over your 401k plan(s) into an IRA for easy tracking and consolidation and to continue the tax deferral status for as long as possible."

#10: Don't Panic, Be Patient. Karen Lee believes one of the most important rules and principles regarding savings is to "be consistent and patient." Davis wants you to avoid the very thing that prevents consistency when she advises, "Don't Panic!!!"

So, whether you celebrate Passover, Easter, or the beginning of baseball season, and whether you'll be watching *The Ten Commandments*, *Ben Hur*, or the original *Planet of the Apes*, you'll want to heed the sage advice offered in these ten don'ts of retirement saving. But enough of this reading the driver's manual stuff. Let's hop into the car and get behind the wheel. After all, no one said you needed to go on the road to retirement by foot. Why not take that fancy sports car you always dreamed of?

In the next chapter, I'll give you the keys…

Chapter Five:
What Drives a 401k to Work So Well

Before we get along too far on our journey to retirement success, let's look at the basic building block to that success — the 401k plan. Rather than relive the history of this peculiar oddity in the U.S. Tax Code, let's focus instead on what makes the 401k vehicle work so well. Indeed, it has worked so well for so many people that we can't ignore its power.

In the simplest of words, a 401k plan can best be described as a souped-up IRA. It's not quite the Shelby of retirement savings vehicles (for those keeping score at home, that would be the SEP IRA), but it does qualify as a muscle car. It performs formidably and, unlike the SEP-IRA, the 401k is almost universally available. So, what makes it tick? More importantly, what keeps this perpetual money-making machine in motion? Find the answers to these questions and you'll discover why the 401k is such a powerful and effective tool for retirement savings.

If you want to get your hands on the key to achieve retirement success, you'll want to fully understand the four primary cogs that drive this magical mechanism. Each of them can offer a vital component to your own quest for retirement comfort. Some of them you can control, some you can't. We'll review them quickly here then delve into each of them in more detail in the remaining chapters of this section.

For the purposes of this overview, and in keeping with our hot rod motif, let's imagine each of these factors as the gears that maximize the potential of all the horsepower the 401k has to offer.

<u>First Gear — Pre-Tax Savings.</u> This is the key motivating factor behind contributory retirement savings plans, whether they be a 401k or an IRA. It's Uncle Sam's way of saying, "Hey, you gotta learn to take care of yourself. Heck, I believe self-responsibility is so important, I'm willing to give you an incentive to get started and keep going."

"By saving in a tax deferred vehicle, the investor is able to defer the time in which he or she has to pay the taxes on the money saved as well as the gains," says Rob Clark, CFP Partner of MPC Wealth Management in Orlando, Florida.

In addition to deferring taxes — and here's the real kicker — pre-tax savings actually cost investors less than saving in an after-tax account. In an odd way, you can give yourself a "raise" (that is, in terms of your net take-home pay) merely by contributing to a pre-tax retirement vehicle. (We'll show you the details of how to calculate this in the next chapter.) I won't go as far as to say saving in a tax deferred retirement plan is like creating money out of thin air, but, given its practical effects, I'm not going to discourage you from believing saving in a tax deferred retirement plan is like creating money out of thin air.

Second Gear — Tax Deferred Compounding. You all know the power of compounding. Well, mix in the tax-deferred element and we shift into a higher gear as this "money that appeared out of nowhere" all-of-the-sudden begins growing at an accelerating rate. By the way, if you want to understand the principle of compounding, think of it as acceleration. When driving a car, as you accelerate, over time your speed increases. When saving in a retirement plan, as your money compounds, over time it grows at a faster pace.

To be honest, many can get along fine just cruising in second gear. Quite frankly, this is where most folks stopped in the early days of the IRA. They'd save their $2,000 a year (that was the limit in the beginning) and plop it into a bank savings account or, if they were daring, a bank CD. They'd do this every year and watch their money grow — slowly, but safely.

With the advent of the 401k plan, we added two more gears, changing our savings vehicle from a '72 Pinto to a '68 Mustang,

Third Gear — Company Match/Contributions. Unlike most IRAs, many 401k plans offer a company match or contribution. A company "match" means the company will match the employee's contribution at a certain rate up to a maximum salary deferral. Most financial professionals will advise employees to contribute at least the amount that maximizes the company's match. Indeed, academic research shows typical deferral percentages cluster around numbers divisible by 5 (i.e., 5%, 10%, 15%) UNLESS the maximum company match is a different number. For example, if the maximum company match is 6%, you're more likely to find deferrals at 6% than 5%.

A company "contribution" means the company will contribute to the employee's retirement account regardless of whether the employee makes a contribution or doesn't. While the purpose of the "match" is to provide additional incentives for employees to save, a "contribution" is often used when an employer seeks to meet minimum annual testing requirements to make sure the plan doesn't treat highly compensated employees more favorably.

In both cases, the money that comes from the company represents "free" money. Unlike the situation in the tax-deferred part above (i.e., "First Gear"), this really is money appearing out of thin air. Grab it. Grab all of it. As soon as you can. Why? It's simple. The company match/contribution shifts your savings growth up a notch as it begins to compound from day one.

Fourth Gear — Investment Returns. Finally, we have the highest gear. Unlike those early IRAs, which often found themselves in slow growth investments at banks, today's 401k plans are supercharged with high-octane equity-based investment vehicles. Unlike bank savings accounts, while they do expose the investor to downside risk, over time they offer the potential for returns far exceeding those of mere mortal bank savings accounts. This difference in returns — even if it were as small as 1% — can have a dramatic impact in the long-term as compounding begins to pump up the value of those returns.

This last gear is usually what gets everyone excited. After all, just as higher gears produce the fastest speeds for cars, one naturally assumes one's retirement plan is growing at a very high rate only because of its investments.

But here's the ironic thing about investment returns: they don't work if there's little to no money in the account. Successful retirement savers have learned that relying on huge investment returns is a fool's game. Indeed, there are no doubt plenty of retirement investors whose investments performed fantastically but who still were left with insufficient assets when it was time to retire. That's because they focused too much on investments and not enough on the single factor that almost always can guarantee success.

Smart retirement investors focus on the right thing. We'll talk about that "right" thing in the next chapter.

CHAPTER SIX:
1ST GEAR: THE RETIREMENT SAVER'S SECRET (AS IN "UNDERAPPRECIATED") WEAPON

When I learned how to drive, we were still required to drive a standard in order to pass driver's education. For those too young to know (or, like me, to care), "standard" refers to a standard transmission, as opposed to an automatic transmission. Most cars today (and even back when I was learning) have automatic transmissions. Automatic transmissions do all the work for you. Standard transmissions require you to work with two feet and one hand, leaving the other hand alone with the steering wheel. (It's a complicated ballet of appendages, leaving one to wonder what would become of cell phones if standard transmissions still dominated the highways.)

I didn't like driving standards when I was a teenager. I figured you only needed to know how to drive a standard transmission if you wanted to race muscle cars. Back then, I had no desire to experience the thrill of attaining high speeds in a few precious seconds.

Back then I was pretty boring.

Nonetheless, I suffered through my training on a standard transmission. I learned one thing rather quickly, once you get into first gear, it's really easy to move into second, third and fourth gears. (The term "four on the floor" refers to a car with four gears and a stick shift in the floor rather than on the steering wheel. That used to be a big thing. Then they invented fifth gear, overdrive and an automatic transmission that nearly equaled those early standards for attaining high speeds in a few precious seconds. How do I know this? Let's just say I got a lot less boring once my father convinced me I really wanted to buy a Camaro Z-28 rather than one of them there "K" cars.)

The trick, therefore, as everyone who has ever driven a standard can attest, is getting into first gear. When initially learning how to a drive standard, I had problems getting into first gear. Lots of problems. You see, with standard transmissions, every time you stopped the car, you had to take it out of gear. Then, to get started again, you had to put it back into first gear. It was during this period that I developed an intense hatred for stop signs, red lights, and the casual pedestrian intent on crossing in front of my oncoming vehicle.

Getting into first gear was tough. Real tough.

But, like I said, after that, it was smooth sailing. Heck, I felt like Mario Andretti taking the standard out on the open highway. It was a feeling that fueled a latent desire within me, one I didn't know even existed.

My father knew, though.

That's why he knew I had to purchase that Z-28. Candy apple red. T-Tops. Everything but electric windows, cruise control, and leather interior. This is not the automobile one pictures the captain of the high school chess team buying, but, after college, that me was long gone.

In the last chapter, I explained how tax-deferred savings represents the first of four gears that drive retirement plan success. In fact, it may be the most powerful driver in the entire set of gears. For some reason, though, the standard method used to encourage this type of savings falls flat with many employees. Why is this such a problem? More important, do you know there's a much sexier way to entice employees to save in retirement plans?

Like driving, getting into first gear is often the highest (and hardest) hurdle retirement savers face. In this manner, tax-deferred savings is both the greatest secret weapon, as well as the most underappreciated weapon, for retirement savers. Like beginning an exercise regime, many people find it hard to even start saving. But, as with exercise, once you develop the habit of saving, it's much easier to continue.

We all know what they say about exercise. It takes time to see the effect, but over that time period, you'll feel a lot better. In a similar manner, the most cited reason for tax-deferred savings also focuses on the long term. Rob Clark, says saving in a tax-deferred vehicle "gives savers the opportunity to have more money working during the time of saving, only paying the taxes when the money is needed for retirement."

There's nothing wrong with this explanation. It is both true and accurate. But, alas, it's about as exciting as watching paint dry. If only there was a more invigorating reason for employees to save. Then they would have a greater interest in the wonders of pre-tax savings. Well, dear reader, a while back I discovered one such reason. Why it isn't used more often I cannot explain, but here it is nonetheless.

Unlike exercise, tax deferred savings can offer the immediate gratification of "feeling good." It can, in effect, give you an instant raise in net take-home pay. Do you think getting an instant raise will make you "feel good"? How about your co-workers? And I don't want to hear a meek "yeah, probably" response. I want you to give me an enthusiastic "Yes! Definitely! And I'm going to give myself an instant raise right now by saving more in my 401k!" response.

Pete Marriott, Managing Director at Trinity Retirement Solutions, LLC in Charlotte, North Carolina, says, "It costs less to save in a tax-deferred account than in an after tax account. That cost is about $0.70 on the dollar to get $1.00 into the tax-deferred account."

"For example," says Dan Palmer, a financial advisor for Rehmann Financial Group in Fort Wayne, Indiana, "a $20 contribution does not cost the employee $20. Because it is pretax it only costs them $15 in take-home pay."

Well, the savings really depends on your tax bracket. Here's how it works. We went to the IRS withholding calculator website and plugged in a few numbers. (For those of you from another planet, the "IRS" is the Internal Revenue Service — that vile branch of government in charge of collecting taxes) Let's say you're a single taxpayer with a $25,000 annual salary, getting paid every two weeks, and with the standard deduction and exemption amounts. According to the IRS site, if you save 5% in a tax-deferred plan, about $48 dollars is taken out of your biweekly paycheck and invested in your retirement plan. However, since this $48 is taken out pre-tax, the amount withheld for taxes falls by $7 from $69 to $62. Because you'll pay $7 less in taxes per pay period, this means your net pay is reduced only by roughly $41, not the $48 that's going into your 401k plan. In other words, by saving $48 per paycheck in your tax-deferred plan, you get to keep $7 more in net take-home pay. Over the course of a year, your annual net take-home pay increases $188 as a result of this tax savings,.

If you're a spendthrift, you're thinking that's an extra latte a week. If you're like me, that's a couple dollars more to pump into the ol' savings account. However, we'd both be wrong. Since that savings includes what we've put away in our 401k, the amount of money we'll have to spend is actually less, but we'll have $188 more of it. I know it sounds weird, but I checked it out and the math actually works. As Table 1 shows, saving in a tax-deferred account is like giving yourself an instant raise.

Now, if you think this is good, imagine if you saved more. Since your tax savings would be greater; therefore, your "raise" — or "net take-home" — would be greater. Remember, your net take-home includes both that portion of your paycheck that you can immediately cash plus the amount you're saving in your tax-deferred retirement account. Using the same example above, if this person deferred 8% of his salary, his net increase in take-home pay would be $300. If he deferred 10%, it's like giving himself a raise of $376 per year. Either way, that's a lot of lattes!

Table 1.
How to Give Yourself an Instant Raise

Deferral Rate	Biweekly Tax Withholding	Total Annual Tax Paid	Annual Salary less Tax	Annual Tax Savings	Biweekly 401k Deferral	Annual 401k Savings
0%	$ 69.54	$ 1,808	$ 23,192	$ -	$ -	$ -
5%	$ 62.31	$ 1,620	$ 23,380	$ 188	$ 48.08	$ 1,250
8%	$ 58.00	$ 1,508	$ 23,492	$ 300	$ 76.92	$ 2,000
10%	$ 55.08	$ 1,432	$ 23,568	$ 376	$ 96.15	$ 2,500
15%	$ 47.88	$ 1,245	$ 23,755	$ 563	$ 144.23	$ 3,750
20%	$ 40.69	$ 1,058	$ 23,942	$ 750	$ 192.31	$ 5,000

Assumes a single taxpayer with $25,000 annual income, paychecks every two weeks, and IRS tax regulations, standard deduction, and exemption amount. Does not include state and payroll taxes.

Source: http://apps.irs.gov/app/withholdingcalculator/

Many plan sponsors struggle to convince employees to save in their 401k plans. They hire professionals to bring out the charts showing how such savings can, over time, grow to impressive sizes. Despite the veracity of these statements, the alluring colors of the graphics, and the fact an experienced professional is often the one stating these truisms, the pitch fails to get the employees to act.

The problem lies in the unfortunate reality of behavioral economics — a bird in the hand is worth two in the bush. People would rather get an immediate reward than a deferred reward worth twice as much. If this is the case, then give them that immediate reward. Tell them the truth. Tell them, by saving in a tax-deferred retirement plan, they can give themselves an immediate raise.

And the more they save, the bigger the raise.

After all, everyone wants a raise, don't they?

But wait! There's more! If you think giving yourself a raise is a good idea, what do you think about getting paid more for giving yourself a raise? We'll discuss that in the next chapter.

Chapter Seven:
2ND Gear: The 401k Equivalent of Cruise Control

So, there I was, motoring down the expressway, refusing to use cruise control. Maybe I'm a control freak, but for a long time I didn't use cruise control. (More likely, I'm a latent techno-phobe, as for an equally long time I refused to use ATM machines.) It takes a lot more effort than you might realize to keep yourself at a constant speed on the open highway. For one thing, getting caught in the traffic of speeding cars makes one naturally increase one's speed to a level one might not be comfortable with. On the flip side, especially when going uphill, it's hard to keep from slowing down.

Cruise control changed all that. Once, we did all the work to maintain our speed. Today, with just a click of the button, you could just sit back and relax. Well, not totally. You still had to monitor the traffic situation. This meant paying attention not only to the cars around you, but your exit ramp and the often changing (where I live, at least) weather conditions. But, all in all, cruise control means your car does a lot of the work for you.

For retirement savers, the power of compounding, most particularly tax-deferred compounding, performs in the same manner as cruise control. Once you get into first gear — once you're saving at the right rate — you'll be amazed how compounding can really rev up your asset growth. Although he never actually said it, it's easy to believe that we attribute to a genius like Albert Einstein the saying, "Compounding is the greatest force in the universe." There weren't any 401k plans around in the days of Einstein. I'm sure, if he were alive today, he would say, "If compounding is the greatest force in the universe, then tax-deferred compounding is a supernatural force."

As alluded to in the previous chapter, most financial professionals use the power of tax-deferred compounding as the leading reason to lure employees to save for their retirement. But, like I said then, people would rather have instant gratification than deferred gratification. Compounding — as powerful as it is (and we'll show its power in a moment) — remains a deferred gratification. People simply must be told first that tax-deferred savings will give them an immediate increase in their net take-home pay. This is the hook that convinces them to save today, right now, without delay. That's why it's called "First Gear." You must do it first to get your retirement vehicle moving.

Of course, once you're comfortably into first gear, then it's time for second gear. That's when we start talking about the awesome muscle of tax-deferred compounding. Traditional compounding alone means earning money on your earnings, not just your savings. "$1 that gets 10% will be $1.10; In year two if you receive 10% it will be $1.21, which will continue for 40 years," says Pete Marriott.

Add to traditional compounding the advantages of tax-deferred compounding, and things really start to swell up.

Dan Palmer, says, "The last item we show is accumulation of those contributions over 30 years. The amount that has come out of their pay is by far the smallest part of the balance. Most of the balance is the match and compound earnings. We have found when we explain it this way to participants that it motivates them to contribute at least up to the match level."

"I have found that in addition to explaining these advantages, an illustration is very helpful," says Rob Clark. "For example, if two investors each saved $1,000 a year for the next 30 years and both earned 8%, the investor with the regular taxable account would have approximately $89,500 assuming the investor is in the 25% tax bracket. While the investor that's saving the same amount assuming the same return in a tax deferred account will end up with approximately $132,000 ($106,800 after taxes on the earnings)."

The following graph depicts the difference in growth between a taxable and tax-deferred account. Rather than use Clark's numbers, we use numbers typical of a 25 year old earning $25,000. Obviously, higher salaries will produce larger benefits than those shown here.

In the sample on the next page, we're looking at the growth of $100 per month contributed to a tax-deferred retirement account and the same amount contributed to a taxable account. The graph assumes an 8% annual return, 4% wage inflation and a 15% federal tax rate. Taxes are taken from the taxable account each month on deposits and annually on gains. You can see, after all this and forty years later (assuming our 25 year old retires at 65), the tax-deferred account has $204,000 more than the taxable account. (At this point, it becomes the CPA's job to make sure the retirement assets are withdrawn at a favorable tax rate.)

Graph 1.
The Advantage of Tax-Deferred Compounding

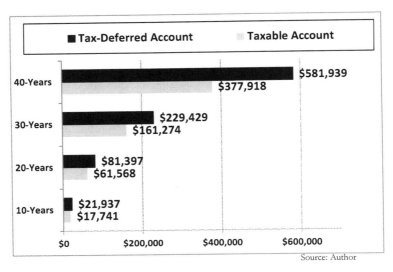

Source: Author

"Over time, compounding can snowball and really add up," says Sandy Arons of Arons and Associates in Brentwood, Tennessee. "The key is to allow enough time to let it go to work."

Lastly, compounding also give us that famous rule, the "Rule of 72." As Arons explains, "To use the rule, simply divide 72 by the expected rate of return. For example, if you expect to earn an average of 8% over time, the Rule of 72 gauges that your investment would double in approximately nine years." Unfortunately, lest you think things are too easy, this rule only applies to lump-sum investments, not periodic investment plans such as those in 401k plans. But it is a close-enough approximation.

We'll see how participants can use compounding to their surprise advantage in a later chapter, but for now, it's important for participants to embrace the idea that compounding puts their retirement savings on cruise control. It makes it easier to attain their goal and becomes more powerful over time.

In a way, tax-deferred compounding is the retirement saver's silent partner on the road to retirement success. We'll talk about a more substantial partner in the next chapter.

CHAPTER EIGHT:
3RD GEAR: TURBO-CHARGING YOUR 401K

Remember that Z-28 I told you about a couple of chapters back? It's one of those rare Camaros that has this thing called "crossfire injection." At the time, I had no idea what the term meant. I'm not sure I know what it means even today. All I know is that it sounds cool. And it works even cooler.

Here's how I would use it. Let's say I was ambling innocently down some country road. There I am comfortably cruising at some sub-light speed, counting the passing cows, taking in the scenery. All of the sudden, some corn field just ahead of me burps out a farm tractor. Though it seemed to burst from the green stalks, as soon as it straightens itself on the road, its speed becomes worse than snail-like. It's that same "watching paint dry"-like slow you experience in those really boring 401k education sessions I mentioned at the beginning.

If you're akin to me, you know how frustrating this is (not just the boring 401k education sessions, but the tractor, too). I naturally nudge towards the center line where I discover I've only got a short passing opportunity. If I don't pass this oozing molasses in front of me right away, I'll be stuck behind it for several more agonizingly slow miles.

This is where crossfire injection comes in handy. I need to pick up speed, and fast. I slip into the passing lane and floor it. Somehow — I know it works this way, I'm just not sure how — my depressing the gas pedal all the way triggers the crossfire injection sequence. Instantly — and unseen under the hood — a valve opens injecting a blast of additional fuel into the combustion chamber. At the same time — and I can see this — the dual flaps on the hood pop open, sucking the fast rushing air into the carburetor to mix with that extra gas. In a moment, the car seems to hesitate before exploding forward under this newfound power.

Within seconds, I'm accelerating down the highway, leaving the sluggish tractor nothing more than a fast-shrinking distant object quickly disappearing in my rearview mirror. During those precious few seconds of maximum acceleration, I have to admit I feel like Luke Skywalker racing through space in one of those X-wing fighters. (I hope this admission does not invalidate my lifetime earned credibility as a Trekker.)

Such is the power and the application of crossfire injection. It's a quick dose of supplementary propellant that allows you to get where you're going a little (or a lot) faster.

The company's 401k match acts just like crossfire injection. And like the loud roar from the engine of my Z28, the company's 401k match is your not-so-silent partner for attaining retirement success. It gives your 401k savings a turbo-boost of free money. As a result, your account will get bigger faster, receive better downside protection, and, finally, increase the odds you will retire in comfort. Ironically, this was not the original purpose of the company match. In fact, you might be surprised to learn that the 401k match, for the most part, has failed to meet its primary objective. As a result, many plan sponsors have reconsidered their matching strategy. This may disappoint some employees, but it makes sense.

With the advent of the 401k plan, plan sponsors sought to transform their traditional profit sharing contribution into an incentive to encourage more employees to save more of their own money. But that's not the only reason why plan sponsors contribute to retirement plans. John F. McAvoy of Waterstone Retirement Services in Canton, Massachusetts, says, "There are three main reasons for an employer match: 1) The company is profitable and those profits would be taxed if not shared with the participants as a match; 2) A Safe Harbor match allows the employers/owners to maximize their 401k contributions; and, 3) A match promotes good will with the employees."

Rick Mason, president of Corporate Markets for ING U.S. Retirement Solutions, based in Windsor, Connecticut focuses on the employee recruitment and retention aspect of the match. "While some plan sponsors offer a matching contribution to take advantage of tax benefits," he says, "most sponsors typically offer a matching contribution to attract and retain top talent at their company. If all other factors are equal, a company that offers a match — or at least a more attractive formula — may be the tiebreaker for many candidates."

Beyond this, though, the company match has become more of a strategy to encourage employees to add to their retirement savings accounts. Rich Rausser, Senior Vice President of Client Services at Pentegra Retirement Services in White Plains, New York, says, "Matching contributions help to motivate employees to participate in the plan. A matching contribution also increases deferral rates among all employees, which improves retirement outcomes and retirement readiness."

Why is it important for companies to encourage their employees to save? Aside from "it's the right thing to do," there are actually compliance reasons why matching is necessary. "It helps with nondiscrimination tests," says Robert Richter, vice president of SunGard's wealth & retirement administration business in Jacksonville, Florida. He adds, "Highly compensated employees are subject to deferral limits that are based on non-highly compensated employee contribution rates. If non-highly compensated employees defer at low rates, then it will limit the amount that the highly compensated employees can defer. Safe harbor plans are a way to eliminate that test, but in order to use the safe harbor provisions the employer is required to contribute to the non-highly compensated employees either a minimum matching contribution or an across-the-board contribution, even for those who do not defer."

The employees, on the other hand, see the company match as only one thing. "An employee matching contribution is free money," says McAvoy. "The match provides an instant return on the savings investment," he says.

Indeed, many financial professionals use the employee match to convince people to save for retirement. "The message is fairly simple: if you don't defer, then you are giving up free money. Where else can you get an immediate rate of return of 50% or 100% (depending on the rate of the employer match)?" says Richter.

There's something more important about the employee match. Like crossfire injection, it provides an inside power boost to the employee's retirement savings account. This can have profound — and positive — implications when the employee retires. "For many Americans, their 401k plan is the cornerstone of their retirement savings," says Mason. Employers who offer the added benefit of a company match as part of their 401k plan are setting up their workforce to be more retirement ready. By offering 'free money' to their employees, it not only encourages participation in the plan, but at a contribution rate that is likely higher than if a match was not offered so that participants are able to take advantage of the match."

As Graph 2 shows, the impact of this "free money" can grow substantially over the decades. In the example here, the employee defers $100 per month and the employer matches 50 cents on the dollar. Over time, the money saved grows at a rate of 8% per year. After ten years, the match produces more than $9,000 in extra savings. After twenty years, the match produces nearly $30,000 in extra savings, more than the employee's total salary deferral. The effect is more pronounced after thirty years, when the match produces almost $75,000 in extra savings, twice the amount of the employee's salary deferral. After 40 years, the match yields $175,000 in extra savings!

Graph 2.
The Impact of Company Matching in a 401k

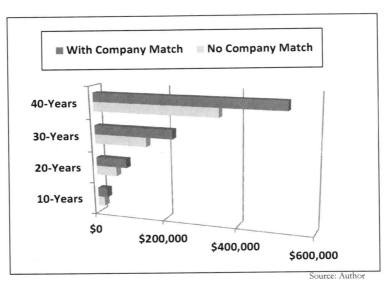

Source: Author

Despite the plain evidence cited in the table, too many employees fail to take advantage of the company match. "Many participants do not understand the long-term compounding affects and how it can change their life," says Michael T. McKeown, Director of Research at Aurum Wealth Management Group in Mayfield Village, Ohio.

The lack of action is particularly acute among younger workers who stand to benefit the most from long-term compounding. "They don't understand it," says Dale Terwedo, an advisor at Terwedo Financial Services, in Edmonds, Washington. "They're young and they're not thinking that far down the road. Sometimes, they also have priorities that get in the way of saving towards retirement."

"Many employees believe they cannot afford to save for retirement," says James R. Peters, author of *The Prosperity Track*. "Unfortunately, those who think they can't afford to save, are exactly the ones who can't afford ***not*** to save for retirement."

Rachel Hawili, Director, Corp. Services at Hefren-Tillotson, Inc. in Pittsburgh, Pennsylvania says, "Employees fail to take advantage of a 401k match because they either don't understand how it works or don't think they can afford to save their own money into the retirement plan."

Jim Sampson, Managing Principal at Cornerstone Retirement Advisors in Warwick, Rhode Island, has a more nuanced take on the reluctance of employees to act on the employer match. He says, "We live in a world of instant gratification, and people are so focused on paying the monthly bills, that a '50-cent match' doesn't get their attention. We need to get back to basics and help folks see how much that '50-cent match' can add up to over time."

At the same time, we're seeing reports that auto-enrollment has been a much more effective way to encourage employees to save. In light of this, some plan sponsors are considering stopping the match altogether. Other research suggests there's a better way. "Behavioral finance studies have shown that sponsors are subliminally telling their employees what to do when they set their defaults," says Sampson. "If they set the match at 50% of the first 6% of pay, many employees will save 6%, because they think that's what they are supposed to do. So if a company is trying to get more bang for the buck on the same matching budget, stretching the match can be very effective. Instead of 50% of the first 6% (which nets the employee 3% of their pay), why not set the match at 30% of the first 10%? Or 25% of the first 12%? The company spends the same 3%, but employees will save more of their pay to receive those dollars. They do need to be concerned with watering down the match too much, because employees may de-value it and not save altogether."

The company match has helped many employees accelerate their savings rate beyond what they could do by themselves. Sampson's concern is well placed. In an attempt to outthink employee behavior, plan sponsors might be taking away a valuable tool that employees have come to rely on. After all, for all its cool appeal, GM stopped producing cars with crossfire injection after only a few years. That's bad news for people who didn't buy cars with crossfire injection, but it's good news for people who did (since those cars are now rarer). In the end, regarding the company match, employees are encouraged to get it while it's still there, for tomorrow it may be gone.

We've still got one more gear. Some say it's the sexiest. You might be surprised by the truth we reveal in the next chapter.

Chapter Nine:
4th Gear: The Final Push that Puts You Over the Top

W e're finally here. After zooming through the lower gears, we've finally made it to fourth gear. This was traditionally the highest gear in many cars. (Though many do have a fifth gear, we're keeping our metaphor to four forward gears.) The top end gear carries with it all the mystique of the open road. You know what I mean: Beach Boys, Jan & Dean, as well as James Dean.

It means fast. It means furious. It means speed in its rawest sense.

It's the deafening roar and multi-colored blur of all those NASCAR machines racing around an oval track.

Are you salivating just thinking about it?

There's only one problem with this popular perception: It's wrong. While it's true you generally cruise at your top end speed while in the highest gear, attaining that burst of acceleration to get to the top end speed is not the function of the highest gear. Indeed, to get the burst needed to pass someone, you might often slip into a lower gear. No, the highest gear has only one objective: efficiency.

Achieving that top end speed requires your engine to work hard. This is usually measured in RPMs. You can hear the strain of this hard work as your engine accelerates. For those of you who share my concern about this strain, you're always worried, waiting for the darn thing to blow. (Yes, this happened to me in real life. Blown engines are not limited to the Daytona 500. And when they blow in real life, it's the end. The end of your trip. The end of getting there on time. The end of the car. So, having experienced the utter depression of a blown engine, you can only imagine the genuine anxiety I feel when the pressure of acceleration starts to make my engine cry.)

How does one alleviate this locomotive stress? By shifting into the highest gear. You see, fourth gear isn't meant to do all those sexy things we think it should do. It's only meant to allow us to pleasantly motor along. It maintains the pace the engine has worked so hard to attain. In the process, it reduces the wear and tear on the engine. It also saves on gas.

But this reality doesn't stop people from block changing gears. Heck, they're so intent on getting to "fast" as quickly as they can they skip all the in-between gears and go straight from first to fourth. Anybody ever try that? How does it usually turn out? Rather than exploding like a rocket, the car more often than not decelerates, whimpering like an embarrassed hound.

It's not unusual for 401k investors to make the same mistake. They're all excited about earning huge amounts that they immediately focus on investing. Investing is not where to begin. As we'll see in Chapter Twenty, like fourth gear, investing isn't as powerful as people think. But it does do one thing. It helps keep you from blowing your retirement engine — but only if you use it right.

Before even trying to understand basic investing concepts, every 401k investor should understand what a mutual fund is. If you already know enough about mutual funds, continue reading. If not, please first read *Appendix I: 8 Basic Investment Concepts Every 401k Participant Must Understand*.

If you must bother yourself with the particulars of investing (again, later chapters will show this is neither necessary nor advised), then you must become intimately familiar with one fundamental concept. Every 401k saver should know this straightforward notion. The trouble is, at many employee education meetings, before making sure everyone is comfortable with this idea, too many advisers too easily slip into industry jargon (you'll get a taste of this a little later in the book). This leaves the typical 401k participant wide-eyed or, even worse, asleep. In the end, without a clear understanding of the plain fact I am about to reveal, the average person will look at investing as a heavy albatross, forever weighing on their shoulders, forever flummoxing their chance for peace of mind.

So, a word of warning to all those brave enough to tread into the morass of investing: Abandon Hope All Ye Who Enter Without a Full Embrace of This Simple Truth: Great Returns Only Come Through Taking Great Risks.

Since the mid-twentieth century, the concept of the relationship between risk and return has represented the cornerstone of investment theory. "Risk and return" are to investing what "supply and demand" are to economics.

But the risk-return relationship did not appear out of nowhere. For centuries, it has been applied in a common sense manner throughout all cultures. Isabella would not have taken the huge risk to her royal treasury had not Columbus convinced her there were riches waiting for the successful voyager. Alexander the Great would not have risked his reputation had there not been a world to conquer. In a story that appears in three different religions, Abraham would not have risked his son's life had the reward of Heaven not been so substantial.

Closer to home, think about the risk-return relationship when it comes to getting paid for doing a certain job. For the most part, jobs that entail more risk also come with a larger wage. This is why coal miners get paid more than bus drivers, who get paid more than janitors. Of course, sometimes the greater pay doesn't justify taking the higher risk. "I like to compare smart risk to silly risk," says Elle Kaplan. "Silly risk is if you offer me a possible return of $200 for crossing a minefield. The reward is not worth it. Smart risk is me crossing a street when the walk signal tells me it is my turn to cross. The risk is small and controlled with returns that are worth it."

Perhaps the most obvious use of the risk-return relationship can be found in casinos everywhere. Most of us know a roulette wheel when we see one. Anyone familiar with the movie *Casablanca* might remember Rick's cold-hearted compassion for the newlywed couple seeking asylum. When they are down to their last three chips, he instructs them to bet it all on 22 — twice. You don't have to be a rank sentimentalist to know that hitting an individual number at the roulette table can pay pretty well. (Hitting it twice in a row after leaving your original winnings on the number can pay even better.)

In fact, mathematically, the reward for correctly guessing the individual number the roulette wheel lands on earns you a payout of $35 for every dollar you wagered. Don't worry about the house, though. The actual odds of guessing the correct number are 38:1 (on an American wheel with a double-zero; 37:1 on a French wheel with no double-zero). So, over time, the house has an average profit of $3 for every $38 bet (well, that's an American house, the French house only has a profit of $2 for every $37 bet, which is a great opening for a French joke, if only I knew one).

How does this show us the relationship between risk and return? It's simple. Compare the relative odds and payouts of guessing an individual number (cited about) against the odds of guessing whether the digit will be odd or even. To keep things easy, and since I don't know French, we'll just reference an American roulette wheel. There are a total of 38 numbers on the wheel, but two of them are zero ("0" and "00"). The rest are numbered consecutively (albeit randomly on the wheel itself) from 1 through 36. This means there are eighteen odd (or even) numbers, so your chances of winning are eighteen in thirty-eight or 9:19. In other words, if you choose to bet "Odd" or "Even," you'll win just about (but not quite) every other time you play. Compare this to a bet made on an individual number, where you'll win once for every thirty-eight times you play.

You can see the "Odd/Even" bet is a lot less risky than the individual number bet. We would therefore expect the payout for the "Odd/Even" bet to be much less than the payout for the individual number bet. Lo! And behold! It is. When your "Odd/Even" bet wins, the croupier pays you one dollar for every dollar you bet. When your individual number bet wins, the croupier, perhaps with less than a smile, pays you thirty-five dollars for every dollar you bet.

Bigger risk. Bigger return.

It's that simple.

Investments work the same way. In the short-term, stocks are much riskier than bonds, but stocks offer much better long-term returns. Likewise, in the short-term, bonds are much riskier than cash, but bonds generally offer better returns. Graph 3 shows this relationship.

Graph 3.
The One Simple Thing
You'll Ever Need to Know About Investing

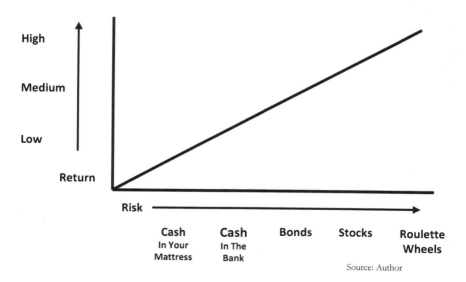

Source: Author

Notice how I sneak in the qualifiers "long-term" and "short-term." These are important considerations. For most, saving for retirement is a long-term process. That, in many ways, is more important than any other investing axiom. "The risk an investor takes when not investing for higher growth is that your investments may not be able to pay for your financial needs in the long term," says Elle Kaplan. "When we retire, our portfolios become our paycheck. Investors should take an appropriate amount of smart risk in order to allow their money to grow to its full potential."

Since the inception of 401k plans there's been a problem of participants being too conservative with their investments. The 2006 Pension Protection Act tried to address this with Qualified Default Investment Alternatives, but investor fears were exasperated by the 2008/2009 market debacle. There are new techniques, however, that can address this age-old question. Vince Allegra, managing director in the Retirement Plan Advisory group at Mesirow Financial in Oakbrook Terrace, Illinois, has found "the best way to create real and meaningful change is through the plan design itself, specifically utilizing features like automatic enrollment and automatic increases." When Allegra comes into a situation where he sees a significant amount of plan assets in fixed instruments, he'll often suggest the plan committee consider a complete plan re-enrollment into suitable default funds.

Andrew Schrage, CEO of Money Crashers in Denver, Colorado, says, "A metaphor that is particularly helpful when explaining the risk-return relationship is one used in the world of physical fitness — no pain, no gain. In order to build a 401k plan with solid returns (the gain), you have to be willing to assume some risk (the pain). I have seen some examples of 401k plan holders being too conservative with their investments. These folks should understand that a 401k plan is a long-term growth vehicle, and especially for those younger in age, the plan will have time to hopefully recover from any short-term losses from equity investing."

It's critical that 401k investors keep their eye on the (long-term) prize and understand how the risk-return relationship relates to their short-term fears and their long-term needs. Unfortunately — and you knew this was coming if you've ever driven a car — there's one more gear. It's not a gear that moves you closer to your goal, though. And that's important to know, because the only protection you have is your own discipline.

I'll talk about this gear in the next chapter.

CHAPTER TEN:
REVERSE GEAR: THESE 401K "BENEFITS" MAY HURT YOUR RETIREMENT READINESS

There are many ways to make mistakes. Too many to list. Some occur out of pure random luck. (Remember the "Nobody Expects the Spanish Inquisition" Rule.) Some occur from our own doing. The worst, though, sneak up on us under the guise of goodness, only to reveal their true malevolence when it's too late to do anything about them.

This chapter is about the latter. In it, we uncover those 401k "benefits" that end up hurting one's ability to achieve retirement readiness — loans, hardship withdrawals, and premature distributions. Not all plans offer these features, but, as we'll see, even that has its own downside. There's no true consensus on the best policy regarding whether a plan sponsor should provide these perks within the plan design. There is, however, one point everyone agrees on: If it's at all possible, avoid using these hidden inhibitors.

Every car has a reverse gear. You often use it to get out of trouble. But you generally don't use it much — only in very specific circumstances. Personally, I avoid using reverse like the plague. Really. I always search for a parking space I can drive through, just so I don't have to back out when it's time to leave. This might be a psychological response to the time, when backing out of the driveway as a teenager — you remember doing that, don't you? — I failed to check my blind spot and knocked over the family basketball hoop; thus, symbolically ending my childhood and putting a dent in my father's new car simultaneously.

Unless you're a Hollywood stuntman, you don't use reverse to drive a car forward. After all, it's not for nothing that they say it's hard to drive by looking at the rear view mirror. For most of us, putting the car in reverse means delaying the arrival to our ultimate destination. Sometimes we take a wrong turn and we have to back up to return to the correct course. Sometimes someone stalls in front of us and we have to back up to get around the obstacle. If we could just go straight to our journey's end, we would avoid reverse altogether and proceed full speed ahead.

The same applies to your 401k. If you'd have your druthers, you'd go full speed ahead to retirement readiness.

Alas, if only 401k plans kept us on the straight and narrow highway the same way IRAs do. You see, unless you're incredibly clever (and, some say, willing to enter into certain grayish areas), you can't take out a loan from an IRA. In fact, unless you're willing to subject yourself to the harsh penalties of Uncle Sam's tax collector, you can't even take out a hardship withdrawal, no matter how "hard" the "ship."

The DOL (Department of Labor, the folks in charge of regulating retirement plans) and ol' ERISA (Employee Retirement Income and Security Act, the law that defines retirement plans) gave us a little bit more leeway than the IRS. It seems, should the plan sponsor think it a good idea, anybody participating in a 401k can take a loan out of it or take a hardship withdrawal from it. During our recent economic doldrums, this has been the difference between some people retaining their homes and the bank foreclosing. That's pretty significant.

There's a growing concern, however, that some employees are abusing this privilege to withdraw prematurely from their 401k account for expenses other than retirement. These withdrawals can range from so-called "hardship" withdrawals to simply taking the money out when employment is terminated. Every such transaction has the effect of delaying retirement readiness.

Financial professionals call these transactions "leakage." "Leakage is where assets leave a 401k plan prior to retirement — where monies are not used for post-employment income purposes," says Jack Towarnicky, an employee benefits attorney in Grandview Heights, Ohio. "Hardship withdrawals are leakage. Post-separation distributions prior to retirement are leakage. Retirement, of course, is defined by each worker, and may include a transition to retirement (flexible or phased retirement), a second career/continued employment, or leisure. On the other hand, loans are generally NOT leakage. The average loan balance is less than $8,000, while the median loan balance is less than $4,000. Most loans are repaid prior to separation (one estimate showed that fewer than 3% of loans are defaulted while employment continues). Most loans that are in effect at separation are NOT repaid and do become leakage (estimates are that 80% of loans at separation are not repaid). One study showed the average loan default was $6,542. However, the total leakage from loans is dwarfed by leakage due to hardship withdrawals and post-separation distributions. Leakage at separation (whether from a loan, or a distribution) is highly concentrated among younger workers and those with very modest account balances."

Towarnicky spoke on the topic of 401k leakage at the 2013 annual meeting of the Academy of Behavioral Finance and Economics. He says that leakage occurs for "many reasons. According to the annual American Payroll Association survey, 'Getting Paid in America,' most Americans live 'paycheck to paycheck' — so that even a short delay in a single check would pose a financial hardship for two-thirds of survey respondents. And, for many Americans, their 401k savings is their only accumulation of cash. So, for those workers who are illiquid and have no ready access to credit, the 401k loan and hardship withdrawal provisions serve as a lifeline."

He says, "One 2009 study showed that about half of all U.S. households reported they could come up with $2,000 in 30 days. Only 33% of those with income less than $30,000 could come up with $2,000 in 30 days. (Where does this $2,000 come from? 50% would source a savings account, 30% would borrow from family or friends, 21% would run up the credit card balance, and 12% would use payday/pawn shop loans)."

While we know leakage can hurt retirement readiness, there could be worse things. Towarnicky acknowledges "leakage creates a hole in your accumulated account balance," but he points out, "with apologies to Tennyson, 'it is better to have saved and lost, than to never have saved at all.' Even a 401k drained by emergency needs is better than the insignificantly higher short term standard of living where no one saves, such that payday/pawn loans must be accessed for such needs."

What can a plan sponsor do to cut back on leakage? "Hardship withdrawals are not subject to Internal Revenue Code § 411(d)(6) anti-cutback provisions," says Towarnicky. "As a result, a plan that previously offered hardship withdrawals can eliminate them. In-service withdrawals and post-separation withdrawals are subject to those tax code provisions; so, prospective changes are necessary. Limiting withdrawals need not create any issue so long as the plan allows loans — and specifically, loans where administration and structure are designed to prompt repayment in almost every situation. My 401k plan eliminated in-service hardship withdrawals in 1996. Participants adjusted easily."

The precise significance of leakage ranges depending on what study you look at. Towarnicky says, "In a 2009 study of 2006 distributions, the General Accounting Office confirmed that leakage after separation is significant ($74 billion), hardship withdrawals totaled $9 billion, while deemed distribution loans (in service loan defaults) accounted for $670 million. At least one study puts the leakage from loans as high as $37 billion annually, although one analysis of this $37 billion number suggests a more reasonable estimate would be $7 billion."

Towarnicky reminds us that "leakage is not a 'plan' issue, but a 'participant' issue. The participant controls the vested portion of the account. So, it may or may not be a 'problem,' depending on the objective to be achieved. Leakage is a problem because Americans have not saved enough for retirement." He feels leakage "ranks a very distant fourth on the list of issues with respect to retirement preparation." Among these, he lists:

1. "Not enough employers sponsor a plan (80 million work for an employer that does not sponsor a retirement plan, Current Population Survey, EBRI), however, many who are ineligible are under age 21, over age 65, self-employed, part time, and low income."
2. "Too many fail to join when eligible (voluntary enrollment rates ~59%, Vanguard, 2012)"
3. "Too many fail to save enough (median deferral rate 6%, median total contribution rate 9.5%, Vanguard 2012)"
4. "Upon separation, 53% of assets remained in the plan, 39% rolled-over to IRAs, 5% was cashed out, and 3% was split between cashout and rollover (Vanguard, 2012)."

While there has been talk among some that leakage is a problem that needs solving, Towarnicky doesn't agree. "My experience is that leakage is an issue for every plan," he says, "particularly leakage after separation, simply because for almost all plans, the only option to access monies after separation is a taxable distribution. More plans need to adopt modern loan processing procedures where participants are able to access funds after separation, in a tax-efficient, electronic loan process (just like electronic bill paying), so those who are not yet of retirement age have access without necessarily triggering leakage."

Leakage is a problem that can be contained at the plan level. But, as I said at the beginning of the chapter, there are a lot of ways to make mistakes. The next section introduces you to the more common — and therefore more easily avoidable — mistakes made by both 401k savers and, sometimes, even by retirement professionals.

SECTION THREE:

– FALSE ROADS –

COMMON MISTAKES THAT RETIREMENT (AND EVEN SOME PROFESSIONAL) INVESTORS MAKE

CHAPTER ELEVEN:
SECRETS FROM THE OLD TOY CHEST: A WARNING TO ALL RETIREMENT SAVERS

There's a famous tale of overenthusiasm (literally "overreaching") told by Ovid in his *Metamorphoses*. You may have heard of it, especially if you're a James Joyce fan. In the original Greek story, Daedalus and his son Icarus find themselves trapped on the island of Crete. Daedalus, a master craftsman, creates wings for himself and his son by gluing feathers together with wax. Before they fly away, Daedalus warns his son not to fly too high, for the sun would melt the wax and the wings would fall apart. Once safely away from Crete, the temptation to fly ever higher proves too much for Icarus. Up, up he goes, until the heat of the sun melts the wax, causing his wings to disintegrate. For all his youthful zest — his overenthusiasm — Icarus falls into the sea and drowns.

For the many like me — (and I can be pretty sure that's a safe assumption because my mother kept the invoice from the day I was born. Under "Item Description" it said "Item: One (1) Standard American Baby (male version) – no contractual or implied warranties") — every Christmas morning you leapt for joy knowing you would soon discover the benefits of being on the "Nice" list. Yes, it's true. No matter what devilish deeds the Standard American Baby undertakes during the previous year, he or she always seems to make it on Saint Nick's "Nice" list. Maybe the Jolly Old Elf is a bit of a push over, or maybe he relies a tad too much on parents' opinions when generating the final list.

Now, I'm sure the previous paragraph made some of you cringe. Before you throw this book down in disgust, keep in mind the times I reference in the above paragraph. I'm from the Charlie Brown era when Christmas was run by East Coast syndicates, and, at the behest of Mr. Macy and his annual Thanksgiving Parade, it was deemed our patriotic duty to consume all sorts of merchandise during the Christmas Season. (For bottom-line reasons, the "Christmas" Season became the brand name of the season encompassing all Judeo-Christian traditional year-end gift-giving celebrations. As such, it was a season much anticipated by Standard American Babies no matter what their race, color, or creed.

Of course, as some of you no doubt remember, it was a time before the invention of the term "politically correct" and when America had a prevailing philosophy directly opposed to the intolerance of "politically correct." Back then, we proudly stood up to non-conformists and declared, "I disagree with what you're saying, but I'll defend to my death your right to say it." And many did. Today, it seems like overenthusiastic non-conformists are more likely to be vilified, sent to "educational training," possibly thrown into jail, and/or, at the very least, have "oh, by the way" problems with their IRS agents.

And that "overenthusiasm" is why we use Christmas as our metaphor. Truth be told, this "overenthusiasm" could apply to birthday gifts, random purchases, or just about any toy that might cause an obsessive reaction from a child. I could have used any one of those metaphors, but only Christmas and the subsequent "politically correct" discussion yields the generally acknowledged dangers of overzealousness in today's political minefield. Such is the magnitude and seriousness of the "over"-reaching problem facing today's retirement savers. While it's not politically incorrect to make these mistakes, the consequences can be just as damaging.

Now, to extend our metaphor: What happens to that toy a child so desperately desires in, say, three months after the child receives it. More than likely, it's been dispatched to the island of misfit toys (a.k.a., "the attic," "the basement," or some distant relative's toy chest). In fact, the greater the overenthusiasm, the quicker the toy disappears into anonymity. After hours and hours of playing non-stop with this same toy, "familiarity breeds contempt" takes over and the toy vanishes from the child's mind, only to be taken up by the next fad.

Sound familiar? Substitute "toy" with "investment" and "child" with "retirement saver" and you begin to see where we're going. Parents know that if they concede to their child's every whim, funding their retirement will be the least of their worries. (To complete our metaphor, substitute "parent" with "plan fiduciary.") So good parents don't spoil their children by giving them everything they want. That is, unless they're very good at selling used toys on eBay.

Plan fiduciaries don't have a metaphorical equivalent to eBay. But they can do some things with plan design to help discourage employees from falling prey to various fads. That, however, is the subject of a different book (q.v., *401(k) Fiduciary Solutions*, Pandamensional Solutions, Inc., 2012). This book speaks directly to retirement savers, for, in the end, the best way to avoid mistakes is to identify them before you're taken in by them. I've broken down these common mistakes into three "over" problems, and "overenthusiasm" isn't one of them. I'll quickly explain their basis in the next chapter before going over each with more detail in the subsequent chapters of this Section.

Remember: sometimes when you reach too high, you get burned. In Chapter Two I wrote "if you are the kind of person who is in a hurry or who thinks they already know everything they need to know about saving for retirement, you're the exact kind of person who MUST read Sections Two, Three, and Four." That sentiment is most true of this section. You see, the mistake described in the next few pages are the mistakes most likely to be made by people who are in a hurry or who firmly believe they know all they need to know.

People in a hurry often find the temptation of short-cuts too enticing to pass by. Each of the three most common "over"-reach errors I write about contain what are called "heuristics." These are decision-making short-cuts that normally permit you to skip all the hard work and due diligence you usually must perform before making life altering decisions. That's exactly the type of thing we're looking for when everyday living finds us squeezed for time. If you ever find yourself making a quick decision by uttering a phrase "sounds good to me," a little yellow light should go off in your head. You may be about to make a mistake, a life altering mistake.

The only difference between people in a hurry and people who think they know everything they need to know lies in their justification. While the former says, "sound good to me," the latter insists "I've already thought about it." Well, it may be true, they may have already thought about it. But, funny thing about retirement saving decisions, the lay of the land often changes. What's good for you in your twenties can be disastrous for you in your sixties.

Your own personal circumstances constantly evolve. That's why, in the final section of *Hey! What's My Number?* where I show you how to monitor your status along the journey to retirement, I strongly suggest you repeat this process once a year. That includes re-reading this entire book. Especially this section. The most common mistakes are most common for a very good reason. Even experienced professionals can fall prey to them. In this one case, I implore you not to be like those experienced professionals.

CHAPTER TWELVE:
THE THREE MOST COMMON "OVER"-REACH
MISTAKES OF RETIREMENT SAVERS

Many new employees can't wait to start investing in their 401k. This might be a good thing or it might be a bad thing. Their overenthusiasm may cause them to take the wrong fork in the road. They might begin studying investments and only investments. As you'll see in the paragraphs in this section, these "studies," even if from reliable sources, can amplify the saver's likelihood of making a common mistake. On the other hand — and this often comes as a result of anticipatory actions of a financial adviser or plan fiduciary — this overenthusiasm can be redirected into a more useful set of actions. (These I've outlined in Section IV.)

Ironically, sometimes a lack of enthusiasm can actually benefit the retirement saver. The market downdraft of 2008/2009 hit retirement savers very hard. The fact the economy had not yet fully recovered five years after the event depressed them even further. Many, like ostriches, just kept their heads in the sand. They even refused to open their statements. They did nothing.

Others felt compelled to "do something." They studied whatever they had to study, even correctly predicting the lack of GDP recovery by the American economy ("Gross Domestic Product" is a measure of the economy's health). They sucked in their collective bellies and sold, knowing (correctly) it would take as long as a decade for the economy to fully recover.

Five years and counting, which group ended up in the better position — the ostriches who lost their enthusiasm or those who reacted with vigor?

According to nearly every report, the folks who kept their heads in the sand did better. Their retirement assets recovered more quickly and they soon returned to the course they had originally set. Unfortunately, those who displayed a certain level of overenthusiasm for action, well, some of them have just never recovered. It turns out it wasn't their overenthusiasm itself that bore the evil mark of "common mistake," but that "over"-enthusiasm made them more susceptible to other "over"-isms that do rise to earn the title "common mistake."

There are three common mistakes that can be classified as an "over"-reaching mistake. They occur when retirement savers are "over"-cautious, when they "over"-diversify and when they're "over"-confident. If you consider each a "disease" (and some psychologists may), then each has several "symptoms" associated with it. These "symptoms" are a lot easier to recognize than their corresponding disease, so don't worry if this "over" stuff doesn't make any sense right now. I'll review the general idea of each common mistake in this chapter. Then I'll identify the specific symptoms in the chapters that follow. For now, here's the quick 4-1-1 on each common mistake:

"Over"-Cautiousness: Did you ever feel like there's no point in taking any unnecessary chances? You just want to sit back and enjoy the fruits of your labors, without necessarily laboring any more to increase the amount of those fruits. I remember, as a Little Leaguer, I had the highest on-base percentage one season. You see, early in the season I discovered two things: 1) I couldn't hit the ball worth a darn; and, 2) Opposing pitchers had a hard time throwing strikes. I did the math and figured the odds were in my favor if I didn't swing. Sure I struck out a few times, mostly when my angry coach yelled at me to swing. But more often than not, I walked. That's what "on-base" percentage means — the percentage of times you made it to base (no matter how) versus the number of at bats you have. Of course, if you don't swing you don't hit home runs. In fact, if you don't swing, you don't hit the ball. So, not only did I get on base the most, I also had the fewest hits. I thought I had out-smarted the game of baseball by playing it safe. Not so. The following season I was cut from the team.

Thus is the evil temptation of "Over"-Cautiousness. You think you can win by playing it safe, but you can't. Ironically, the only way to play it safe is by taking a chance. Without taking a chance, you're pretty much dooming yourself to failure. Look at all those "over"-enthusiastic retirement savers who sold off after the 2008/09 market crash. They thought they were playing it safe. Little did they know they ended up taking the biggest chance of their lives — and they lost.

"Over"-Diversification: It seems like "Don't put all your eggs in one basket" is an adage burned deep into those brain cells devoted to decision-making. Something to do with Mark Twain and all. And since Mark Twain is the American Paragon of "Common Sense," we just gotta do what the guy says. Right? Well, if you want to do what Mark

Twain advises, I have a surprise for you. He never said "Don't put all your eggs in one basket." What he really said was "Put all your eggs in one basket — and watch that basket!" Think about the wisdom of this. We've all got only so many hours in the day. With limited resources, we can watch only so many baskets. Isn't it better to concentrate on just one basket instead of all those many baskets?

By the way, this is one of the first (and often last) tragic mistakes made by entrepreneurs. They start a business and think they can take over the world. They accumulate customers like it's going out of style — until they figure out they just don't have the capacity to serve so many clients. They can study all they want about "distribution bottlenecks" and such, but by then, it's too late. Service begins to suffer, clients leave, and the entrepreneur's reputation is scarred. (I first discovered this lesson when my grandfather refused my suggestion to increase the market share of the family pizza stand at the Erie County Fair — by that's another one of my book's — *A Pizza The Action.*)

I learned it again as it pertains to the business I'm in when I saw the best sales reps for the company I was working for realize, because they hit their personal capacity limits, they would only tread water for the rest of their careers. They soon quit. And, when I started my own business, it was predicated on being modestly profitable by serving to the max only a limited number of clients. In many industries, and especially the service industry, "boutique" business plans like this often work. It's only when companies grow beyond their niche that many begin to fail.

The failed companies, in essence, made an investment decision to diversify, not a business decision to vertically or horizontally integrate. While it's not a guarantee of success, the business-based decision is usually more successful than the investment-based decision. The same is true for retirement savers. They regularly fail to realize their decision to broaden the holdings of their portfolio leads to "Over"-Diversification. This is just about as useful — and possibly just as harmful — as buying too much insurance. After all, how many times can you die and how much money does your family really need when you do die. It's a finite amount. Once you exceed that finite amount, the premium costs are no longer adding value, they're hurting your current cash flow. You'll have to work more hours to maintain your standard of living. If you think selling your soul to the company store is bad, just think how much worse it is to sell your soul to your favorite insurance agent.

"Over"-Confidence: Every so often, you just "know" your beloved sports team is going to win. There can only be one inevitable outcome in such a situation: It will all end in tears. Now, I'm not saying this just because I'm a Buffalo Bills and Buffalo Sabres fan. Each year, in any given league, only one team can win it all. That means the season will end in tears for fans of all the other teams. It's part of what being a fan is all about. It's that irrational confidence that your team will go undefeated every year. ("Irrational?" Yes. After all, the word "fan" comes from "fanatic"). I hate to break it to you, but unless you're the 1972 Miami Dolphins (and that was only due to a controversial fumble call against those same said Buffalo Bills), it ain't gonna happen.

By the way, long suffering sports fans in Buffalo may have discovered a cure for this "it will all end in tears" phenomenon: when it comes time for the playoffs, we cheer for any team playing against the team from Boston and/or the surrounding New England Region.

You want to know the worst kind of "Over"-Confidence when it comes to sports fans? Those who are absolutely confident they're right, and have the statistical evidence to back them up. Don't you just love to see those guys lose to your fantasy team? Funny thing about that. It is this same overreliance on statistical measures that causes retirement savers to succumb to the common mistake of "Over"-Confidence. What is this strange fascination with numbers and, in particular, statistics? Even Einstein said, "God does not play dice with the universe." In the investment field, this "Over"-Confidence derives from an old theory that held markets are "efficiently rational." In other words, the idea was that people — a.k.a., investors — will always make rational decisions. When several anomalies began to appear in the theory, all the finance professors and all the Wall Street rocket scientists couldn't put it back together again.

Finally, from a once-shunned field called "behavioral economics" came this simple question: What if man doesn't make decisions rationally? That turned out to be the key. Once we removed the assumption of rationality, a lot of these anomalies were easily explained. Still, some stick to the old theory or its remnants. The lure of "Over"-Confidence is just too big to ignore. But the cost isn't.

Perhaps the most famous modern example of "over"-reach occurs in the movie *Indiana Jones and the Last Crusade*. In deciphering his father's book, Indiana Jones discovers the Holy Grail. But there's a catch. He can't take it with him. When the evil Nazis try, the ground splits and the Grail nestles itself on a ledge just beyond reach. The beautiful Nazi agent Elsa believes she can reach it, but when she tries, she falls to her death. Indiana then nearly succumbs to the same temptation, but, unlike Icarus, heeds the wise words of his father who warns Indiana to stop. As he retreats, Indiana looks back to the old knight in the background, who nods his head approvingly, as if, again, saying, "You have chosen wisely."

When designing plan menus, a good fiduciary will be careful to create them in such a way as to mute the alluring music of these common mistakes. Ultimately, it is the responsibility of each individual retirement saver to "choose wisely" and avoid being over-cautious, over-diversified, and over-confident.

I'll explore the most obvious symptoms of these common mistakes in the next six chapters. In the meantime, I'll leave you with this: When is it better to ignore "common" sense and plunge full speed ahead? Turn the page and the answer will be revealed.

CHAPTER THIRTEEN:
3 (BAD) REASONS 401K SAVERS
ARE OVER-CAUTIOUS

In 2006, Congress passed the Pension Protection Act. Among the objectives of that legislation was to address several major problems then occurring within 401k plans. One of those snags dealt with retirement savers' tendency to be too cautious with their long-term investments. I call this common mistake of retirement investors "Over-Cautiousness." It means sacrificing long-term return for short-term "safety." You'll see why I put that last word in quotes a few paragraphs from now. First, a few facts you might be interested in knowing.

According to "401(k) Plan Asset Allocation, Account Balances, and Loan Activity in 2011," (*ICI Research Perspective*, December 2012, Vol. 18, No. 9), in 2002, (prior to the 2006 Pension Protection Act), only 40% of 401k plan assets were placed in equity funds. In 2007, this number rose to 48% (still not as high as the market peak in 1999 when 53% of 401k assets were held in equity funds). Following the market debacle in 2008/09, 401k equity fund holdings dropped to a low of 37%. As of 2011, and despite the market recovery, only 39% of 401k assets are invested in equity funds. This means a large segment of 401k investors have missed out on these returns, making it harder for them to meet their retirement objective.

Why is this so? What can be done to prevent this?

Bad Reason #1: "My Feelings are Hurt."

David Rae, Vice President of Client Services with Trilogy Financial in Los Angeles, California, says, "Investors often make investment decisions based on emotions ranging from euphoria to fear. In this past recession many people moved all their 401k holdings to cash, generally out of fear. If you are sitting in an interest-bearing account and earning less than the inflation rate you are losing money with no chance of coming out ahead. They've also missed the big market recovery many have enjoyed the past few years. On the way up, they often buy, buy, buy with euphoria, which often leads to panic selling when things go south. So many people are stuck in a buy high, sell low pattern. I talk to many people who have no idea that the stock market has gone up the past few years."

What are the "killer emotions" exhibited by retirement savers that lead to this behavior? "The biggest killer is watching the financial media and having a crisis-to-crisis investment prospective," says Craig Morningstar, COO at Dynamic Wealth Advisors in Phoenix, Arizona. He says, "investing is a life-long experience, from the day we save our first dollar, until we pass-away…or run out of money."

Bad Reason #2: "Fool Me Once…"

Over-cautious retirement savers exhibit very specific symptoms that investment professionals and plan fiduciaries can often spot right away. For example, Morningstar says one symptom is "following the short-term industry performance rating." This, he says, is caused by retirement savers "chasing returns and looking at data with less than 5 years of history."

Ozeme J. Bonnette, Financial Coach at Tri-Quest Investment Advisors in Fresno, CA, agrees, pointing out, "Many investors were overly aggressive to begin with. They were chasing returns or hot sectors in an effort to ride the market up, but were not prepared for the large downside that is possible with an aggressive portfolio."

Though burned by their own misplaced enthusiasm, retirement savers don't look at themselves as the problem. Instead, they blame the market, make that, the "tricky" market, or "those evil Wall Streeters," or whatever the class warfare term *de jour* happens to be. They thus become cautious, leery of having been taken in by a market that "fooled them once."

Bad Reason #3: "Safety First."

Savers look at the short-term, especially after market collapses like 2008/09, because they revert to a "safety first" mentality. "For many retirement plan investors, this is their life savings, no matter how large the account," says Bonnette. "They do not have other savings accounts, emergency funds, or other investments to fall back on. Many of these investors are over cautious because they cannot afford to lose anything. The first sign of a drop in the market causes them to go into protection mode to try to salvage what is left."

Unfortunately, simple math explains why this approach is actually dangerous to retirement saving. Bonnette says, "Being overcautious to the point of moving to cash in a down cycle leads to a very high probability of not recouping losses. Most investors move to cash when the market drops, hoping to get back in when the market is on its way back up. Unfortunately, no one has truly succeeded in timing the market. By the time investors realize the market is rising, it's too late to catch the huge wave."

Why is it so hard for retirement savers to understand how "Safety First" hurts them in terms of long-term investing? "Safety keeps investors safe in the short-term," says Morningstar. "Most investors do not have a long-term perspective. The only way to have a confident long-term perspective is to be investing for years....since childhood. Without that experience, the investor needs to understand and believe the numbers. Safety has a cost most retirement plan investors don't realize."

"So, What's the Cure?"

"One cure for over-cautiousness," says Bonnette, "is working with an advisor you trust to help you determine whether the investment's performance is just a reflection of the state of the market or if there are actual quality issues that require one to sell and reinvest elsewhere. Many retirement investors have such a hard time understanding this because many are not financially savvy. Some don't have access to information. Others don't take the time to utilize the resources that are available. I have seen a noticeable difference in the performance of the accounts of clients who I work with when I compare those I meet with regularly to those who choose to work on their own."

Rae says, "Individual investors are better off working with advisors for a few reasons. Most importantly they can help the investor determine how much they need to be putting away to accumulate enough assets to retire. Even if the investor has a crystal ball and picks the best investment available in their plan, but fails to save enough, that investor still won't be able to retire. An advisor is also there to help you avoid the slew of other mistakes that investors make that greatly decrease their odds of becoming financially independent."

For those unwilling or unable to work with an individual adviser, Morningstar believes the best way to cure the problem of over-cautiousness comes down to this simple rule: "Don't look at the short-term media."

It's important for 401k plan sponsors — and anyone else acting in a fiduciary role — to understand why retirement savers become over-cautious. In this way, they can better construct 401k investment education seminars to deprogram this common mistake from the minds of employees. Still, you shouldn't rely on your employer to tell you how to avoid this mistake. I'll repeat this *ad infinitum*: You are solely responsible for your retirement success. The safety trap snares so many unsuspecting retirement savers because it conforms to our normal predisposition to avoid danger. We can blame evolution for this.

Long ago we learned it was better to sleep in trees. Why? Because lions can't climb trees. Eons of the fittest surviving has programmed the cranial mass within our skulls to act safely. That's just not an easy thing to up and throw away. It takes an inordinate amount of discipline to redefine "safety" as it pertains to retirement saving. It's not an impossible task, but it is a challenge. I'll tell you one thing that makes it easier to accomplish: knowing you must do it in order to retirement in comfort.

You now know it.

For you, avoiding the mistake of being over-cautious just became a lot easier. Congratulations!

But there's no rest for the weary, for as soon as you learn to avoid being over-cautious, you'll need to address the next "over" abundance. This one poses an even greater trial, for it flies in the face of one of the most repeated adages in the history of investing. If you've ever read Samuel Clemens' *Pudd'nhead Wilson*, you already know what I'm talking about. If you haven't, the next two paragraphs will reveal the answer.

CHAPTER FOURTEEN:
OVER-DIVERSIFICATION AND THE 2 LEAST UNDERSTOOD INVESTMENT RULES THAT MOST HURT 401K SAVERS

Now, I know I said investing isn't important, but I recognize some of you still insist on giving it your attention. We've seen how over-cautiousness falsely leads 401k savers to invest in "safe" options that end up not being safe. It turns out other "common sense" behaviors actually work in an opposite fashion than expected. We can blame this counter-intuitive sense on a lack of understanding of some very mundane investment basics. If only 401k savers really understood these basics, they'd be less likely to commit errors that may hurt their chances for a comfortable retirement.

Here's another one of those basic misunderstandings that seem counter-intuitive. We've all been told of the importance of avoiding placing all our eggs in one basket. This appears to make sense. After all, if anything ever happens to one basket, we still have several others to count on. What they don't tell you is the cost of this strategy. Think of it this way. Say you have to hire a "basket" guard for every basket you own. That can get expensive, especially the more baskets you own. Pretty soon, the value in the basket equals the cost of the guard. This questions the entire strategy. It echoes Mark Twain's previously mentioned advice. Here it is in full from his novel *Pudd'nhead Wilson*:

> *Behold, the fool saith, "Put not all thine eggs in the one basket" — which is but a matter of saying, "Scatter your money and your attention"; but the wise man saith, "Pull all your eggs in the one basket and — WATCH THAT BASKET."*

This translates very easily into the world of investing. First, as we'll discover in two chapters, we know academic research suggests the optimal portfolio size is between 30 and 50 stocks (for an advanced look at the academics, see *Appendix II: "A Trip Down Memory Lane – Revisiting Portfolio Optimization"*). Beyond this number, the cost of diversification tends to eat away at the portfolio's investment performance. This leads to the first reality that most 401k savers must deal with — the average number of holdings in the typical mutual fund far exceeds this optimal portfolio. This means, even if 401k investors were to select only one fund, chances are they would already be over-diversified.

But it gets worse.

Too many 401k savers assume they must diversify among mutual funds, forgetting that mutual funds themselves are already diversified portfolios. We define "Over-Diversification" as the tendency to buy too many mutual funds, thus creating a high-fee index fund. (An index fund is an unmanaged portfolio that simply contains every stock in a particular index of stocks. The S&P 500 is perhaps the most famous index.) Why do so many retirement savers believe they should buy more than two to three mutual funds, which in themselves are already diversified portfolios?

"Because there is limited transparency and knowledge that similar funds hold the same investments," says Craig Morningstar. "Most retirement plan investors are told to buy more funds, and they have no way to know there is an overlap of holdings."

Tad Hill, president of Freedom Financial Group in Birmingham, Alabama, says, "The issue of over-diversification doesn't get explained to people very well. This is especially true if all of their savings are inside of a 401k plan. There may be no one giving them any education on how to allocate their portfolio."

"It all comes down to context," says Gabriel Potter, Senior Researcher, Westminster Consulting, in Rochester, New York. "Investment consultants have been banging the drum of the benefits of diversification for decades, so it's not surprising that some investors have absorbed the lesson but misapplied it." Potter asks that, since "investors have been sold on the idea of diversification, isn't having more than one fund better as well?" He points out, "The drawbacks are obvious to professionals, but require a little thought."

Unfortunately, many 401k plans have been designed to automate processes that lead to these naïve diversification strategies. "Many 401ks are set up to have online service and management of the portfolio by the individual, removing one-on-one advisor interaction or discussion," says Amy Rose Herrick, an investment adviser representative and Agent in Christiansted, US Virgin Islands. Does this sound like your 401k plan? She continues, "On the website, generally a few questions are answered to determine a preset 'model.' The investor elects a model. Using the model, selected assets will be divided into a percentage-based distribution among multiple funds. If offered, investors may pick a target date fund (i.e., balanced portfolios that automatically adjust their investments based on a specified retirement "target date") instead of a model. Perhaps a metering device will show if a fund is low risk, moderate, or high risk in some visual format. However, this does not mean that either election the client has chosen to use will be the right answer. Clients using any of these methods will likely not be able to identify if the downside risk is within their tolerance levels either. I feel this design assumes all investors are well informed and know exactly what they are selecting. It is my opinion that this is far from reality."

To address these design failures, many 401k plans are moving towards a one-portfolio solution. These "lifestyle" funds, not to be confused with the popular target date funds which are based on your expected (i.e., "target") retirement date, are like traditional balanced profit sharing plan portfolios, which are based on the traditional (eg., "aggressive," "moderate," "conservative") risk spectrum of investment choices. As such, they represent a single portfolio managed towards the needs of the plan demographics. Typically, there is a single option default fund meant for 401k investors who want to concentrate on saving and not worry about making an investment decision.

"There are a number of advantages towards simplifying a portfolio," says Potter. "First, this is simply the application of limited returns — adding more funds to a properly diversified portfolio will only have a marginal impact. Second, there is a finite amount of time allotted for due diligence — simplification allows for greater depth of understanding instead of spreading this time between too many funds. Third, as already suggested, combinations of managers often (unintentionally) counter-act active bets. Manager A's actions may offset the active bets of Manager B — in other words, you'll end up with combined passive performance at active fees. ('Passive' refers to index funds, which generally have lower expense ratios because they do not pay professional analysts to pick stocks like 'active' funds do.) Finally, adding more options can add to indirect costs because of extra accounting, error checking, as well as the aforementioned direct costs."

Morningstar agrees. He says, "If the single portfolio can produce better results than a self-designed portfolio, all the better for the plan investor. Improving better outcomes is where the true focus should be, which is different than just higher returns."

These "one-portfolio" single options differ from target date funds in that they are not managed to a theoretical retirement date but to a consistent demographic. This bypasses the confusion related to "which date are we talking about: retirement or death?" Again unlike target date funds, "one-portfolio" funds rely less on asset allocation models and more on traditional investment management. ("Old time portfolio management. Just like Edie Shore. And Ben Graham.")

Of target date funds, "the asset allocation models used to construct these portfolios are not necessarily congruent with what we would call prudent investing," says Patrick Hejlik, CEO, Fourth Quadrant Asset Management in Danville, California. "They are based on historical preferences and data on what someone who is 'x' years old 'should' have and this could be based on faulty assumptions." For example, imagine two fifty year olds. One has no savings outside his 401k plan and the other has a large savings and an even larger inheritance coming. Under the Target Date Fund scenario, they would both be placed in the same age-based fund; hence, they'd receive the same asset allocation. Their personal circumstances, however, suggest they might be better served by different asset allocations. In practical terms, this means it's in their best interests to have a plan with risk-based as opposed to age-based fund options.

If you're not familiar with the term, "asset allocation" takes the idea of diversification within stock portfolios and spreads it out among different asset classes. The three most widely known asset classes (in order of which have the best long-term investment returns) are stocks (or "equities"), bonds (or "fixed income") and cash. Through the years, the industry has broadened the definitions of asset classes to include such things as real estate, precious metals, commodities, and even into subclasses of existing classes like, in the case of equities, large-cap, mid-cap, and small-cap stocks. It seems like nowadays, almost anything can be called an asset class and, thanks to the proliferation of investment products and sales distribution channels, almost everything is.

The core concept of asset allocation states that if you diversify among assets you can reduce your downside risk. Unfortunately, twice in the last ten years (2002 and 2008/09), the market collapse consumed all asset classes, leaving both professionals and the average investor to wonder if asset allocation is dead. "Investors got burned on asset allocation models in 2002 and 2008/09 because the underlying assumptions on how the assets would behave in a downturn were faulty," says Hejlik. "This is a common problem when using historical data to make asset allocation models and using securities that are not designed to profit when markets become dislocated."

Potter says, "Diversification is a necessary component of portfolio construction, but it is insufficient to protect against all types of risk." "We might argue that investors who were truly honest with their consultants about their genuine risk tolerances have been reimbursed over time for the market downturns in 2002 and 2008/09. Rather, we suggest a scenario-based analysis for generating an investment policy and the discipline to apply it is more important. However, if investors believed that asset allocation alone was sufficient to protect them from precipitous drops in their portfolio balances, the past decade has been a painful lesson in the limits to historically driven models and Modern Portfolio Theory ('MPT')." [N.B.: More on MPT next chapter.]

Andrew Wang, Portfolio Manager and Senior Vice President at Runnymede Capital Management, Inc., in Mendham, New Jersey, sums up what all 401k savers should know: "The industry preaches the benefits of diversification so most investors desire to own more than two or three mutual funds. Most advisors aim to balance risk through asset allocation by owning all major asset classes such as cash, bonds, stocks, real estate, and commodities. In theory, each asset class has different levels of risk and return and is supposed to create a portfolio of uncorrelated assets, meaning that when one went down, another went up. However, in [2002 and] 2008/09, virtually all asset classes moved in tandem, and they declined in unison."

Like the proverbial elephant in the room, it comes down to these two basic investment facts: 1) The optimal portfolio size is 30-50 stocks (well below the average number of holdings in a typical mutual fund; and 2) The reputation of asset allocation appears to have suffered during the worst years in recent history. Some professionals believe it makes sense for the average 401k saver to consider the "one portfolio" approach as the most efficient solution to the investment question.

For two generations, MPT has been the prevailing investment theory. Although it has come under fire recently from both academics and practitioners, it remains the "generally accepted investment theory" according to the Department of Labor. For this reason, many professionals still bow their reputation at the altar of asset allocation. In the interest of fairness and open-mindedness, let's take a common sense look at the evolution of investment theory in the next chapter. Read it if you feel it's important, but let me warn you, you may be very surprised and even upset with the way the story ends.

CHAPTER FIFTEEN:
EXPLAINING 401K INVESTING
THROUGH THE LENS OF HISTORY

Ford? Chevy? Is there really a difference? For some strange reason only the marketing gurus of Madison Avenue can explain, hordes of people have a cult-like attraction to a particular brand. Some people prefer Fords. Others would swear by their Chevys. Still others, unfortunately for the UAW, prefer foreign makers. But a car is a car is a car. They pretty much all feature a steel-frame chassis sitting on four wheels with an engine, a fuel tank, and a comfortable cabin area for driver and passenger seating. Yes, they come in different sizes, different colors, and different styles, but they all achieve the same purpose. No matter what make, model, or class, all cars will get you from here to there. Some a little bit faster than others, but they'll still get you to where you want to go.

And, just like cars, there are a lot of investment styles out there. You can choose different asset classes like stocks, bonds, and cash. Heck, just within the stock class alone, you can pick between growth or value, between active or passive, and/or between foreign or domestic. But you know what? It pretty much doesn't matter what style you pick, they all get you where you need to go.

OK, that's not totally true. There are investments that are inappropriate for long-term investors. Hopefully, your retirement plan sponsor or other adviser has pointed these out and, in the case of a 401k plan, limited their availability on the plan menu, or, in the case of your own IRA, your adviser has told you they're inappropriate.

So a better way of commenting on your menu of investments is to say, among the *realistic* choices available to you, they'll all get you where you want to go. Some may take a little longer than others, but in the end, you'll be fine.

Now, I need to admit the following: The above statement has gotten me into a lot of trouble with my investment adviser friends. And I empathize with them. As an investment adviser, I've had to pick one investment style to focus in. (Not that it's relevant, but in the interests of full disclosure, I picked Ben Graham's value style.) Understand this: when an adviser chooses an investment style, he doesn't merely casually opt for it, he becomes an ardent advocate for it. There are many legitimate reasons for this, but such is this passion that many advisers possess a missionary zeal to convert all prospects towards their particular style of management. That's like a Ford dealer trying to tell a life-long Chevy adherent to buy a Mustang instead of a Camaro. (Again, in the interests of disclosure, I'm a life-long Ford guy. The only reason I bought the Camaro was that, in 1983, the Mustangs just weren't what I pictured a muscle car to be.)

A fiduciary, on the other hand, always does what's in the best interests of the client. That means, if that Ford dealer were a fiduciary, he wouldn't be concerned about selling Fords to all people, only those who in their best interests could use a Ford. Now, that doesn't mean the Ford dealer shouldn't try to sell the Ford to a Chevy fanatic. It could very well be that Chevy fanatic might not realize a Ford would serve his best interests. In fact, ideally, a car dealer would offer any make of car. In this way, the dealer could provide the most appropriate make to the customer.

In the same way, an adviser serving in a fiduciary capacity understands that different clients would best be served by different investment styles. Of course, the difference between selling cars and making investment decisions is that you can sell any make, any model, at the drop of a dime. On the other hand, it takes a good portion of your working career to garner enough experience to be good at any particular investment style. That's why it's so difficult to nimbly switch styles. And that explains the source of the missionary zeal. Imagine spending a good portion of your life heading down a particular highway only to realize you might be going the wrong way. It's not easy to accept you're wrong. In fact, it's only natural to argue everyone else is going in the wrong direction. But that's a behavioral finance thing. We don't need to get into that particular psychology topic in this book.

Which brings us back to the dilemma of all investment advisers. What must they do to insure the client's best interests are always served? If that fiduciary doesn't provide the right investment style, then, as a fiduciary, he would need to direct the client elsewhere. That's a tough nut for many advisers to swallow, but that's what a fiduciary does. Always in the best interests of the client. Never in the best interests of the adviser. That's why it's often difficult for a great salesman to also serve as a great fiduciary.

So, for both investment advisers and for people prone to invest (like retirement savers), it makes sense to have a keen understanding of the different investment styles, what makes them different, and the type of investor each style might be more appropriate for. Let me make this clear: the following doesn't advocate for any particular style. It's meant merely to highlight some of the differences. Which style is in the best interests of each investor depends on that investor.

Let's begin with the short happy history of the evolution of investing.

A terribly unexpected thing happened on Tuesday, October 29, 1929, so terrible that that particular day has become known as "Black Tuesday." OK, maybe it wasn't that unexpected. Maybe this was one Spanish Inquisition we should have expected. The warning signs had been there for weeks. Perhaps it was our own hubris. (Keep an eye on that word "hubris." I guarantee you'll see it come up again and again.)

After pressing stratospheric highs into the late 1920s, the actual market decline began in September of 1929. It continued into early October before the selling frenzy started in earnest on Friday, October 18th. The first "Black" fall occurred on, appropriately named, "Black Thursday," October 24th. There were some feeble attempts to settle things down (along with the usual Black Helicopter theories as to why these attempts failed), but the following Monday (also given the moniker "Black"), saw a far greater drop. Panic selling had set in. Then, on Black Tuesday, the bottom fell out. (Oddly, Black Monday saw a greater percentage drop than Black Tuesday, yet the 29th gets all the credit.)

One thing the 1929 stock market crash shouldn't get credit for is the Great Depression. It may have accelerated the economic calamity, but most cite the policies of Hoover and Roosevelt as the prime reason the American economy fell into the abyss. This doesn't mean the crash wasn't indicative of significant problems within the capital markets themselves. There were, and, to his credit, after a few earlier stumbles compounding Hoover's mistakes, Roosevelt led the way in truly stabilizing equity exchanges. In a flurry of activity, the government created The Securities Exchange Act (two of them in fact) laying the groundwork for the markets as we know them today.

"The Securities Exchange Act of 1933 (33 Act) was designed to provide some basic rules of engagement, level the playing field, and assign some accountability to protect investors," says Vern Sumnicht, CEO of iSectors in Appleton, Wisconsin. "The objectives of the 33 Act were to require that investors receive all material information about securities being sold and to prohibit fraud, deceit, and misrepresentation of information. To accomplish these objectives, the 33 Act requires disclosure of important financial information through the registration of securities. This is to allow investors to make informed decisions. The 33 Act provides for accountability by giving investors who purchase securities and suffer losses important recovery rights if they can prove there was incomplete or inaccurate disclosure of important information."

The 33 Act was followed immediately by a similar act in 1934 and by the dual Acts of 1940 that set the adviser industry framework: the Investment Company Act of 1940 and the 1940 Investment Advisers Act. While Washington was firming up the rules, leading financial thinkers of the day were trying to formulate ways to study individual stocks, rank individual stocks, and determine the best time to purchase individual securities. In case you're wondering, this was the onset of the era of individual security analysis. Benjamin Graham, who, together with David Dodd co-authored the seminal book *Security Analysis* in 1934, has been ordained the Father of Value Investing.

"Value investors seek investment opportunities to purchase assets at a discounted value and hold them until the market realizes their inherent value and the price of the asset appreciates," says Liam Timmons, President of Timmons Wealth Management in Attleboro, Massachusetts. "Value investors often focus on companies with low valuations (relative to historical levels or peers or the market overall) where the current value of the company is below its long-term potential. Oftentimes, this can mean buying companies that are undergoing short term operational challenges, management changes, or are struggling with newly emerged competition where the belief is that the market is overreacting to short term issues or vastly underestimating the growth or earnings potential of the company."

A competing form of securities analysis quickly countered the popularity of value analysis. While there is no clearly recognized "Father" of growth investing, one of the early practitioners was Philip Fisher, author of *Common Stocks and Uncommon Profits*. Originally published in 1958, the book remains popular today. Companies that can be classified as growth stocks "usually include visible growth in earnings, revenues, and share price," says Nicholas V. Ventura, President & CEO at Ventura Wealth Management in Ewing, New Jersey. "Investors who seek 'growth companies' often forgo traditional valuation metrics. Examples would include social media companies that have a wide reach but little in terms of profits. Chased for quick return, growth companies that fail to deliver in revenue or profit are often punished terribly in market corrections. Since no one really knows what the growth will be they are often the first to be cut from portfolios in a market rout."

Graig P. Stettner, a Financial Advisor at Strategence Capital, Fort Wayne, Indiana, says value investing offers an advantage when "stocks that are despised by investors get assigned, by virtue of their prices being depressed, lower than average valuation multiples, reflecting investor pessimism. When the pessimism abates, there is a re-rating higher of the stocks' valuations." Likewise, he says there's an advantage of the growth style "in that there are certain times when the economy is not growing and the tide is not lifting all boats. In those times, a growth company/stock may deliver what the average stock is not able to deliver, a rising stream of sales earnings. It is at times like these that a growth style may be in favor."

For decades following the Second World War, advisers would debate the relative merits of growth versus value investing. Adam D. Koos, President and Portfolio Manager at Libertas Wealth Management Group, Inc in Dublin, Ohio, says, "Value investing is like going shopping for clothes and heading straight for the sale racks: high quality, but low cost. Growth investing is like shopping at the trendiest store with no regard for price, hoping that everyone will buy the same shirt you picked up off the display model."

Many traditional securities analysts see the capital markets as the ongoing battle of two great forces: Momentum and Reversion. "Growth investors tend to focus on momentum, believing that companies growing faster than their peers make better investments, and that the stock price is of lesser importance," says Tom Weary at Lau Associates LLC in Greenville, Delaware. "Value investors tend to focus on reversion, believing that all companies revert to the mean over time, and thus that it is better to buy troubled companies' cheap stocks in the hope that both operating performance and valuation return to average. The danger comes in over-emphasizing either. A growth investor can overpay for a stock that then stumbles, causing a collapse in the stock price. A value investor can try to 'catch a falling knife' where a cheap stock gets cheaper as things unwind at a company."

Falling kitchen utensils aside, while this value vs. growth debate continued unabated, a new theory blossomed from the notes on one of Harry Markowitz's napkins. Ultimately labeled "Modern Portfolio

Theory" (or "MPT"), it would challenge the very assumption of security analysis, regardless which flavor — growth or value — you preferred. The ascendency of MPT led to a more portfolio-centric, rather than an individual stock-centric, emphasis. By focusing on portfolios instead of individual stocks, statistics, not accounting fundamentals, became the dominant metric. This, in turn, led to the popularity of index funds (a.k.a., "passive investing"). "Since investing is a zero sum game — for every winner there must be a loser — you have a 50% chance of winning from the get go," says Bradley Roth, President at Kattan Ferretti Financial in Pittsburgh Pennsylvania. "However, you must add management fees, commissions, trading fees, taxes, etc. After you are done, most active management styles underperform. If low-cost passive investing is done correctly, using proper diversification and rebalancing, passive investors are likely to beat the majority of active investors over time. Passive investing will also eliminate many harmful emotional decisions. Historically, emotion tends to be the major contributor to underperformance. By eliminating 'market timing' emotional decisions, investors are already ahead of the curve."

The debate therefore shifted from "value vs. growth" to "active vs. passive." Timmons says, "The key advantage of passive investing is lower costs and removing manager-associated risk from investing. By keeping costs low and seeking to track an index, investors can be better positioned to achieve average market returns over the long term. Strong bull markets where correlations are high among stocks can favor passive investing." Alternatively, he says, "The key disadvantage of passive investing is the lack of downside protection; if you believe the market is not fully efficient and manager skill can steer a portfolio away from bad companies or risky investments during market turmoil, active investing can be positioned to provide better returns in declining markets. Passive investing can appeal to investors seeking to keep costs low and that lack the time or training to select active managers."

Today, we may be seeing the beginning of the debate between domestic vs. foreign securities. These debates are ongoing and, evidence would suggest, constantly shift. A good fiduciary is aware of all styles of investments, their advantages and disadvantages, and the types of investors each might be more appropriate for. "There is no 'one size fits all' retirement plan," says Elle Kaplan. "Investment style is complex and needs to take into account all of your financial goals, your current financial state, the risk you're willing to take, the nature of the markets, what kind of a time frame you're working with, and more. Assess your long-term goals (what age do you want to retire? what do you hope your life in retirement will look like? what are your legacy goals?), plan for your expected future needs, and build in room for unanticipated expenses. You would never just hop into your car without a clear idea of how to get to your destination. The key to a secure and happy retirement is to have a detailed road map that will help you navigate the terrain and get you where you want to go. That way, you can be sure to live out the retirement of your dreams."

With this in mind, the challenge comes when the rubber finally meets the road and disciplined decision making is required. "The most frustrating experience I have had comes with convincing 401k participants to have patience and avoid chasing returns," says Heather MK Wonderly, Senior Consultant at AKT Wealth Advisors LP in Lake Oswego, Oregon. She says, "'Rearview mirror investing' never pays off, but behavioral studies show it is extremely difficult for people to resist this temptation. Some of my larger retirement plan committees have chosen to stuff the genie back in the 401k bottle and only offer professional investment management to their employees. While this can be a wonderful solution for some, others find it to be too difficult politically."

When it comes to research, though, we need to remember one thing: Of the three most important components to successfully achieving a comfortable retirement outlined in Chapter Twenty, investments are nowhere to be found. Still, retirement savers cannot willfully ignore investment selection, since there are several dark paths one can inadvertently venture down. For this, we need to rediscover the world before the ascendency of portfolio-centric thinking. For that world reveals a truth that stands to this day. That truth comes alive in the next chapter.

Chapter Sixteen:
Over-Diversification and the 401k Saver – Too Many Stocks Spoil the Portfolio

How many stocks do you need to hold to avoid over-diversification? What's the point of holding hundreds of stocks when all it becomes is a proxy for the market? Indeed, Warren Buffet has said, "I cannot understand why an investor would put money into a business that is his twentieth favorite rather than simply adding more money to his top choices."

We all know the success Warren Buffet has had holding only a handful of companies, but does his strategy sufficiently reduce unsystematic risk? (In case you're wondering, "unsystematic risk" is a fancy term that means buying poor performing stocks instead of the stocks that perform well. "Systematic risk, on the other hand, refers to what happens when the entire market drops.) Oddly, the prevailing academic literature supported Buffet when he began to accomplish his above average performance returns. Back then, only a handful of stocks were necessary to be considered sufficiently diverse. Today, the academic consensus appears to be roughly 30-50 stocks (2001, Campbell, J.Y., M. Lettau, B.G. Malkiel, and Y. Xu, "Have individual stocks become more volatile? An empirical exploration of idiosyncratic risk," *Journal of Finance*, 56, 1-43 and (2010) Hicham Benjelloun, "Evans and Archer — Forty Years Later," *Investment Management and Financial Innovations*, Volume 7, Issue 1, 2010, pp 98-104).

But how does this impact the real world of 401k savers? Would they see better returns if their mutual fund options were limited to portfolios of 30-50 stocks? I looked at this question for an article I wrote for *FiduciaryNews.com*. I sought to answer these compelling questions by using the Morningstar database (performance through 8/31/11). First, I screened for all no-load domestic large-cap equity funds with no 12b-1 fees and a "growth objective." I then ran one filter that gave me a list of all mutual funds with fewer than 50 stocks ("Optimal Holdings") and another filter that gave me a list of all mutual funds with more than 500 stocks ("Over-Diverse Holdings").

I found the average mutual fund in the Optimal Holdings category held 36 stocks. With an average Beta of 1.02, it appears these portfolios came very close to mimicking the risk of the market (which has a Beta of 1.00). If this sounds Greek to you, then you should know "Beta" is a term professionals use to measure a portfolio's "risk" (actually, "volatility", which is another issue altogether and one that we'll get to briefly in Chapter 19 and more deeply in Appendix IV). Over 5, 10, and 15-year reporting periods, the average fund in the Optimal Holdings category beat the S&P 500 by 1.20%, 0.93% and 0.23% respectively. So, these funds outperformed the market despite having a similar market risk profile. Incidentally, as an aside, the average Gross Expense Ratio (the cost of operating the fund) was a whopping 1.68% — and they still performed significantly better than the index.

Of course, this is an unfair comparison because I'm comparing actively managed funds to an index and, as Warren Buffet has demonstrated through the years, during certain market cycles it's often easier for smartly run actively-managed funds to beat the index because they don't have to buy the poorer performing stocks the index is required to contain. Be careful, though. I'm not saying this is true for all actively-managed funds, just those astutely run and during certain market cycles.

Instead, I'll compare this set of actively managed funds against other actively-managed funds, in this case the Over-Diverse Holdings category. In the Over-Diverse Holdings category, the average fund holds 730 stocks. Oddly, despite the larger amount of holdings, the average fund had a Beta of 1.06, indicating slightly more market risk versus the Optimal Holdings average. Over 5, 10, and 15 years, the average Over-Diverse Holdings fund respectively underperformed the market by 0.23%, beat the market by 0.29% and underperformed the market by 0.47%.

Comparing these two groups, the funds in the Optimal Holdings category (roughly 50 stocks in their portfolios) consistently performed better than the funds in the Over-Diverse Holdings category (those with more than 500 stocks in their portfolios). Over a 5-year period, Optimal Holdings beat by 1.43% annually. Over a 10-year period, Optimal Holdings beat by 0.64% annually. Over a 15-year period, Optimal Holdings beat by 0.70% annually. Again showing the folly of looking at the expense ratio of a fund (yet another thing we'll get to shortly), the average Gross Expense Ratio for the underperforming Over-Diverse Holdings category was only 0.62%. This is more than 1% cheaper than the average fund in the better performing Optimal Holdings category. Sometimes you do get what your pay for.

Remember, this is no mere academic study; these are actual portfolios with real track records. Granted, this is only a snapshot-in-time and the Morningstar database reflects a "survivor bias," (since poorer performing funds are often closed and therefore removed from the database) but presumably the survivor bias would benefit both categories. After all, we're not comparing the results to an index.

Thirty or so years ago the interest in optimal portfolio size peaked. At that time, the issue of trading costs made it difficult to create portfolios with large numbers of holdings. In fact, investors once understood the foolishness of buying a handful or so of mutual funds for the sake of "diversification." They then knew the dangers of building portfolios consisting of hundreds of stocks. These virtual indexes have lagged considerably behind actively managed portfolios in recent years. As a result, there is a greater need for 401k investors to know to ask the question, "How many stocks do you need to hold to avoid "Over-Diversification?" Not only should this alert the 401k plan participant to the potential dangers of owning multiple mutual funds, it should also guide them towards selecting the appropriate fund.

Perhaps Warren Buffett gives us the answer when he says, "Diversification is protection against ignorance, but if you don't feel ignorant, the need for it goes down dramatically." (Lenzer, R. "Warren Buffett's Idea of Heaven: I Don't Have to Work with People I Don't Like." *Forbes*, October 18, 40-45, 1993.)

The portfolio-centric view stole our eyes from paying attention to "the ball" of long-term growth — an essential necessity of all retirement savers. It led to rampant Over-Diversification within 401k investments and likely caused poorer returns than traditional "one-portfolio" profit-sharing style investments that emphasized a security-centric view. Among leading plan sponsors, the pendulum of consensus is swinging away from the false promise of the portfolio-centric view, and is returning to focused portfolios with fewer stocks, similar to what Warren Buffet advocates.

Having tackled the common mistake of Over-Diversification, let's not get too cocky. There remains one more "over" bearing emotion that hurts 401k investors. This is perhaps the most frightful demon of them all, for it has Greek tragedy written all over it. We'll discuss this vile temptress in the next few chapters. Read on, but only if you dare, for, if you are human, you've likely been victimized by this trait.

CHAPTER SEVENTEEN:
DETECTING THESE SIGNS OF OVERCONFIDENCE CAN HELP 401K INVESTORS AVOID A FALL

Hubris. It's the one tragic flaw of every Greek hero. It's often mistaken for mere arrogance, a fatal trait if there ever was one, but it's much more than that. It's an extreme form of pride that causes one to exaggerate one's abilities. As with all things Greek, hubris extends well beyond the healthy moderation of self-confidence into the unrealistic illusion of invulnerability. The tragedy, to borrow from Shakespeare, is when hubris causes a hero to be "hoist on his own petard." Metaphorically, the Bard has Hamlet turn the tables on his enemies through this metaphor of having the bomb maker blown up by his own bomb (petard). This is what hubris can do. It also represents the third of three "over" mistakes retirement investors should try their best to avoid.

We've already covered "Over"-Cautiousness and "Over"-Diversification. This third common investor mistake comes from "Over"-Confidence, a.k.a., "hubris." It's the polar opposite of "Over"-Cautiousness. Whereas "Over"-Cautiousness keeps people from buying during historically low markets, "Over"-confidence keeps people from selling during historically high markets. Both reactions suffer from what behavioral scientists call "recency" — i.e., the propensity to overemphasize the most recent phenomena and extrapolate near-term data well beyond its tendency to return to the mean.

"Over"-Confidence infects both amateur and professional investors, although many will say professionals are more likely to be "Over"-Confident and amateurs are more likely to be "Over"-Cautious. It can manifest itself in many ways. One example of "Over"-Confidence is relying on a theory far beyond its ability to successfully predict outcomes. This occurs when such theories move from the category of theory to that of myth. Brian P. Beck, President & CFO at Wealth Management Group of North America, LLC in Farmington, Connecticut says, "'Simple' rules, rules of 'thumb,' canned investment advice from 'financial advisors' on TV, can really hurt an investor in the long-run. Investing is not an exact science and no one has come up with the 'perfect' investment strategy, not even Warren Buffett."

For example, there was once a theory that said funds with lower expense ratios (remember, this is a number reflecting the cost of operating the fund) produced better returns than funds with higher expense ratios. It turns out this is only true for index funds, not actively traded funds (which represent the greater bulk of the fund universe). Indeed, the previous chapter provides just one very specific example where the investment returns of funds with coincidentally higher expense ratios far surpassed the returns of lower expense ratio funds with a similar objective. This doesn't imply there's a correlation between high expense ratios and above average performance returns, it just proves there's no universal truth to the lore that low expense ratio funds always produce higher performance returns than high expense ratio funds.

Ozeme J. Bonnette says "There are so many myths about which funds are better or worse than others. They are often all misleading, whether the myth relates to high versus low expense ratios or index versus active management, for example. Expense ratios are only one element of the analysis. The bottom line is that investors have to compare apples to apples. One can't compare an international fund to a domestic fund, or a bond fund to an equity sector fund. Compare funds against their peers and their respective benchmarks. Understand the management and the management style. Know how the managers are being compensated. (Will they get bonuses for besting their peer group, which may lead them to take chances with their investments?)"

The DOL (again, that stands for "Department of Labor") hasn't made it easier for 401k savers, either. The DOL's 401k Fee Disclosure Rule, without a template approved by the DOL, leaves the participant looking only at the data out of context. Despite the DOL's warning not to look at fees alone, participants will look at fees alone — for better or worse. David Rae says, "I've run into quite a few people who have almost their entire 401k in company stock often because it has no fees. While I do believe you need to consider fees when looking at investments, that shouldn't be the only way you pick an investment. Bottom line, it's not what you make but what you keep. The net of fees number is way more important than just the basic fee being paid."

Thankfully, most people don't have to worry about investing their retirement money in company stock, a form of "Over"-Confidence 401k participants are most susceptible to. This kind of hubris leads you to invest a disproportionate amount of your retirement savings into the stock of the company that employs you. Not a good idea. Chris Chen, of Insight Financial Strategists, LLC in Arlington, Massachusetts told me a tragic tale we should all pay attention to. "In the case of my client, he was fully invested in the company stock, and would not diversify away because he thought that it was too good of an opportunity to pass up. Eventually when the stock price peaked, he had nearly $1 million in the company stock in his 401k. Then the stock started sliding, and sliding. When he finally got out of it, he had $50,000 left. To rub salt in the wound he was laid off. Eventually the company filed for bankruptcy."

The more widely understood example of "Over"-Confidence is the simple refusal to believe "no tree will grow to the sky." You begin to hear this phrase more often when the market approaches historic highs. People begin to create ever more fantastic (i.e., unrealistic) scenarios to justify not selling. As a result they stay in the market straight through its most precipitous drop. This happened to many people at the end of the dot-com bubble in 2000-02 and at the end of the real estate bubble in 2008-09.

Notice what one word appears during both of those periods – "bubble." A growing bubble is a sign of "Over"-Confidence. The one problem, though, and the reason so many people believe "this time it's different," is because it's terribly difficult to predict just when a bubble will burst. Furthermore, market cycles tend to complicate any analysis. One style of investing (e.g., growth) might see its stock prices rise during a bubble while another style of investing (e.g., value) remains undervalued. This is what happened in the 2000-2001 period. Growth investors, who had their salad days in the late 1990s, drew negative returns for three straight years (2000-2002). Value investors, while lagging (but not negative) in the late 1990s, found they had positive returns in 2000 and 2001. (Just like the 2008/09 market debacle, nobody escaped the Post-9/11 market decline in 2002.)

Perhaps the best way to avoid being a bomb maker who is blown up by his own bomb is to avoid being a bomb maker in the first place. For 401k savers, this may mean relying on either direct or indirect investment advice from a professional. Rae says, "An advisor is also there to help you avoid the slew of other mistakes investors make that greatly decrease their odds of becoming financially independent."

Hubris will tell us of the sweet smell of our own sweat (or some other bodily function). It can also make us think we can outsmart the market. Neither is true. But it does reveal how awful hubris can be. For you see, the word "petard" derives from the Latin *peditum*, which means, uh, shall I say, "to break wind." Indeed, the word Shakespeare actually wrote — petar' — wasn't cut off merely to appear poetic. It was purposely used as a pun for a word that in those times meant flatulence. And, with that, if you didn't realize how unbecoming "Over"-Confidence was before you read this chapter, I hope that etymological fact will stun you back into reality.

Hubris, then, relies on the sweet smell of otherwise foul myths to lead us astray. Let's take a look at two popular myths that have all the markings of Over-Confidence. Bear in mind, you might not be aware of these myths. You can, however, as Groucho Marx might be tempted to say, "bet your life" savings (and many do) that the industry sneaks these myths into their advertisements in such a manner that they seem undeniably true. Heck, so cock-sure are these claims that only a fool would question them.

Well, the next two chapters will give you enough ammunition to join me in being the next Don Quixote (whose epitaph closed with the line "to live a fool and die a sage"). Just promise me this: When questioning someone on these myths, don't bring out the heavy ammo until you've set them up properly. String them along just far enough so they have enough rope to hang themselves. Then hit them with the common sense data you are about to discover.

CHAPTER EIGHTEEN:
MUTUAL FUND EXPENSE RATIO MYTH BUSTED

In his book *You Are Here: A Portable History of the Universe*, Christopher Potter devotes an entire chapter to the dilemma of measurement, both in the sense of astronomy universe and the atomic universe. This quandary confronts and, ultimately, may confound even our smartest scientists. Why? No matter how hard we try, we tend to base measurements on arbitrary and often purely convenient references. So, while technology allows us to measure more precisely, the relevancy — or, more aptly, the irrelevancy — of those measurements haunt the dark shadows of the brightest minds. Should we use a yard or a meter? Fahrenheit or Celsius? The solar year or the lunar year? "The choice of measurement units," explain the scientists, "merely reflects a scalar translation."

One of the most pervasive myths in the investing universe — and one that impacts the world of 401k savers the most — involves mutual fund expense ratios. A mutual fund's expense ratio is the percentage of the fund's total net assets that is consumed every year by the fund's total annual operating costs. The performance return numbers of mutual funds already include the effect of a fund's expense ratio. The myth I would like to address in this chapter states that "lower expense ratio mutual funds perform better than higher expense ratio mutual funds." Like all absolute statements, this one is grounded in a partial, but by no means universal, truth. It gained national media attention when an August 2010 Morningstar study, "How Expense Ratios and Star Ratings Predict Success," concluded that lower expense ratio funds did better at predicting mutual fund success than Morningstar's star rating system. The study went as far as to say, "In every single time period and data point tested, low-cost funds beat high-cost funds."

That's a pretty strong statement, but is it true? It's not clear Morningstar still seems to think so. As recently as its June 2011 Investors Conference, Laura Lutton, editorial director at Morningstar Inc., said, "Cheaper funds are far more likely to outperform." ("Morningstar exec Laura Lutton: Stick with Cheaper Funds," *Investment News*, June 8, 2012). There's a reason why scientific researchers like to use hedging language such as "far more likely" rather than absolutist assertions like "in every single time period" — it's too easy to knock the absolutist off his pedestal.

Inspired by my son's avid watching of the popular MythBusters TV show, I decided to borrow their "question authority" attitude and try to whack this dangerous myth off its podium. Since Morningstar represented one of the dots connected to the "Low Expense Ratio is Better" myth, I figured what better place to get my data than the famous mutual fund rating service itself. I took a look at their August 31, 2012 data disk and ran a screen for all index funds with a best fit benchmark of the S&P 500, that were true no-load funds, that weren't feeder funds, that had no short positions, and that had either a "growth" or "growth and income" objective. This produced 50 funds (well, actually 51, but one was a "bear" fund meant to perform opposite of the S&P 500, so I threw that one out). I then ran several different scatter graphs like these two and, once you removed the noise, they looked remarkably similar:

Graph 5. S&P 500 Index Funds Annual Returns (2011) vs. Annualized 10-Year Returns (ending 2011)

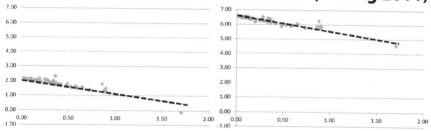

Source: Morningstar

In both cases, the scatter graphs appear near to what the theory predicts. The implied regression line (the dotted black line) is sloping downward, indicating a negative correlation between the expense ratio (on the x-axis) and the total return (on the y-axis). Indeed, the correlation in both sample sets is -0.92. In a situation where lower fees would always mean higher returns, the correlation would be -1.00. This is pretty close, but, as you can see, there are several data points showing cases where higher expense ratios correspond to higher returns. Still, while not supporting the August 2010 Morningstar study's "every single case" language, these results remain consistent with Lutton's "far more likely" remark. This makes perfect sense. All S&P

500 index funds like the ones shown here contain the same stocks in their portfolios. This therefore produces the same baseline performance in all funds. The only real difference in the actual returns of different funds can then only be due to different expense ratios. It looks like this myth may be true — at least in the case of index funds.

Unfortunately for this theory, however, the universe of active funds proves to be not a very happy place. Using the same base Morningstar data disk, we ran the same screen, changing only the requirement that the fund be an index fund to the requirement that the fund not be an index fund. This produced 110 candidates (again, after removing a "bear market" fund). As you can see, the resulting scatter graphs look nothing like the index fund graphs above. In fact, you might say these graphs put the "scatter" in the scatter graph.

Graph 6. Large Cap Active Funds
Annual Returns (2011)   vs.   Annualized 10-Year
Returns (ending 2011)

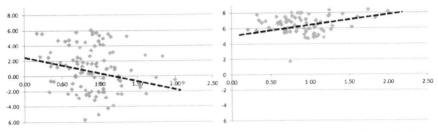

Source: Morningstar

In the case of these actively managed funds, the scatter graphs show plenty of examples where higher expense ratio (x-axis) funds produced better performance (y-axis) — the exact opposite conclusion of the August 2010 Morningstar Study. Indeed, the correlation of the Annual 2011 Returns was much less (-0.18) while the correlation was actually positive for the 10-year data (+0.16). This positive correlation may be an artifact of survivor bias, but that doesn't remove the fact that plenty of high expense ratio funds earned higher performance numbers than their less expensive counterparts.

While expense ratios may be important when conducting due diligence on index funds, they may be less important — and even misleading — for actively managed funds. Therefore, it would not be unusual to find a high expense ratio actively managed fund with better investment returns than a low expense ratio actively managed fund.

This myth gets really dangerous when people (regular investors and professionals alike) use the "low fees are better" mantra to compare funds across different asset classes. Years ago, when the DOL first proposed that 401k plan sponsors give preference to lower fee funds (in line with this myth), I gave them a call. I asked them, "Since when is the DOL in the business of giving investment advice?" The speaker on the other end of the phone of course denied the Department was giving investment advice. I went on to explain their suggested language demanded plan sponsors select the lowest cost funds. At the time, the lowest cost funds were bond index funds. "Therefore, according to your very own language," I told the spokesman for the government regulator in charge of retirement plans, "you are telling people to place retirement assets in the worst performing long-term investment."

There was a pregnant pause on the other end of the line. It was followed with a curt "No we're not!" I'm sure this faux pas struck home. I'm equally sure I wasn't the only one to bring up this irony in their proposal. You see, they had just won a major battle in Congress to do something about all those retirement investors who required long-term returns but were hurting themselves by investing in bond funds instead of stock funds.

Let's not get too upset with those vendors selling bond funds (at least not for this reason). I believe the real culprit in perpetuating this myth are the index fund salesmen. Why? Because index funds (which don't require any active portfolio management at all and therefore don't incur the cost of hiring someone to study stocks) have the lowest fees of them all. Let's take one more look at two of the four scatter graphs we saw earlier (see below).

Graph 7. Annualized 10-Year Returns (ending 2011) S&P 500 Index Funds vs. Large Cap Active Funds

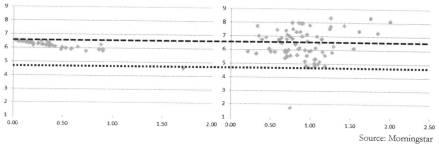

Source: Morningstar

In the ten-year period ending in 2011, the highest performing S&P 500 fund averaged 6.54% per year. Coincidently, that particular S&P 500 index fund had the lowest expense ratio (0.02% or 2 basis points) among all S&P 500 index funds. The heavy dashed line represents this high point for S&P 500 funds. I've stretched this line across and through the second graph, which represents actively managed funds with a similar objective as an S&P 500 fund. As your eyeballs make it clear, about half of the actively managed funds beat the best index fund. This is about what you'd expect in a typical performance-reporting period. The challenge, of course, is to identify which half will outperform the index. Answering that question is beyond the scope of this book (although I can say there are plenty of financial advisers out there more than happy to help you come up with the answer). It is within the scope of this chapter to tell you the one thing not to base your guess on: the actively managed fund's expense ratio. Take another look at the above graphs. You'll see that Graph 7 reveals five out of the six active funds with the highest expense ratios all beat the best (and lowest expense ratio) S&P 500 index fund.

Since we're on the subject, the worst performing S&P 500 index fund yielded a paltry 4.56% annual return. Not surprisingly, it had the highest expense ratio among all S&P 500 index funds (1.71% or 171 basis points). More surprisingly, all but one of the actively managed funds (and, of course, one on the lower end of the expense ratio) handily beat the poorest performing S&P 500 index fund. More broadly, the median actively managed fund out-performed the median S&P 500 index fund (6.33% vs. 6.24%). This occurred despite the index funds having a median expense ratio only a third of the median expense ratio for active funds (30 basis points vs. 89 basis points), Sometimes you get what you pay for. (Where'd we see that before?)

And regulators echo this sentiment. The SEC (which stands for the Securities and Exchange Commission, i.e., the government arm that regulates mutual funds) doesn't say to stick to low expense ratio funds, it merely (correctly) points out, "As you might expect, fees and expenses vary from fund to fund. A fund with high costs must perform better than a low-cost fund to generate the same returns for you." (www.sec.gov/answers/mffees.htm). Along the same lines, the DOL also stipulates that fees should only represent part of an overall analysis of the appropriateness of an investment.

Alas, limiting ourselves to the written word, we cannot bust this particular myth with the fanfare of brilliant (and loud) pyrotechnics, but the results are nonetheless the same for every alert 401k saver: as your eyes can plainly see from the actual data presented in the scatter graphs, this myth is busted.

See. Wasn't that easy? I hope you understand just how easy it is to stretch a kernel of truth into a seemingly "universal" truth. That's what makes the sales side of any industry earn those big bucks. As a consumer, though, you need to be aware of this common trick. In the case of the myth that it's always better to go with the lowest price mutual fund, hopefully you've got some good examples of why (when, and where) this often doesn't work. If you're interested in learning more about the fees that really matter, feel free to go to the back of the book and read *Appendix III. Fees that Really Matter.*

Myths involving numbers are easy to either prove or blow up. Because it's so plainly quantitative, the analysis rarely leaves room for a Spanish Inquisition surprise. The next chapter — the longest and by far the most controversial in *Hey! What's My Number?* — introduces a myth that is one of the hardest to refute. It is a conceptual — or "thought" — myth. Likewise, "thought" experiments (a.k.a, "words") provide the only way to confirm or deny these myths.

Worse, the myth we are about to tackle starts with a common sense idea that has been morphed into a fundamental principle of investing for more than half a century. People don't take too kindly when you start tearing away at fundamental principles. Well, too bad for those people. The worst kind of Over-Confidence is the "they've been doing it for years" argument. It contains not one but two logical fallacies. The first is the (by now familiar) appeal to authority (the "they" part of the argument). The second is a form of an appeal to the masses (in other words, "if everybody is doing it, then so should I"). I'll leave it to your mother to tell you the problem with that argument, but I'm sure you remember, at one point or another, your mom using the ol' "if all your friends jumped off a bridge, would you?" retort. And you won't believe the reason people give in the next chapter for jumping off that bridge.

Chapter Nineteen:
RISK ISN'T WHAT THEY TELL YOU IT IS.

"Bomb patterns?" General Peckem repeated, twinkling with self-satisfied good humor. "A bomb pattern is a term I dreamed up just several years ago. It means nothing, but you'd be surprised at how rapidly it's caught on. Why, I've got all sorts of people convinced I think it's important for the bombs to explode close together and make a neat aerial photograph. There's one colonel in Pianosa who's hardly concerned any more with whether he hits the target or not."

- *Catch-22*, Joseph Heller.

Like many nerdy science types, I spent my high school days rebelling against English class. I despised reading anything but pure science (a youthful fault long overcome). The hatred of any and all works of fiction rose to such a fever pitch that in 10th grade I convinced a dozen or so of my classmates to simply refuse to read a novel and write a report on it. The teacher countered with a refusal of his own — he refused to give us a passing grade unless we completed the assignment. At least that was his initial response. Upon reflection, he decided to give us a choice. We could either read a novel and write a report on it, or we could write our own novel.

The burden of writing an opus overwhelmed my peers, and they chose to merely report on someone else's work. I, on the other hand, possessed (and continue to possess) a head of such rock-hard stubbornness that I considered my teacher's directive not the false choice he intended it to be, but a command to write my own novel.

And so I did. It was called *Armageddon* (yes, the same name as a Bruce Willis movie — but my geo-political thriller had nothing to do with asteroids crashing into the Earth. If I ever find the manuscript I'll publish it and you can see for yourself.)

One of my other high school pet peeves was this unending (and rather inane) debate as to which was the better novel: Joseph Heller's *Catch-22* or Kurt Vonnegut's *Slaughterhouse Five*. Both had recently been made into movies and both carried the same satirical anti-military flare popular during the Vietnam era (think of their contemporary — and much more popular — film *M*A*S*H*). It was considered more "hip" to side with *Slaughterhouse Five* in this dispute, so, naturally, having read neither book nor seen either movie, I championed *Catch-22* as the better. I've since read both and my position hasn't changed, although I do admit I, like many others, prefer Vonnegut's style. But you have to read his entire canon to come to this conclusion and *Slaughterhouse Five*, considered by many to be the culmination of his writing, cannot stand alone.

When I finally came around to reading *Catch-22*, of all the elements that struck me, none has stuck in my mind longer than the phrase "tight bombing patterns." First, the visualization of this thought comes across clearly. It's even easier to picture if you've ever watched actual footage from a World War Two movie that shows the bombardier's view of his ordinance exploding in a straight line through some unfortunate city-grid far below him.

That straight line is a "tight bombing pattern." In *Catch-22*, the dysfunctional generals preferred the perfect portrait of a tight bombing pattern above all else. At one point, if memory serves correct, an award was given to the flight crew that managed the tightest bombing pattern. The celebration of this award ignored the fact that the pilot ordered his payload dumped into the sea, long before his plane reached its target and long before the pilot would have had to dodge and weave between the deadly flak fired from below. In the topsy-turvy world of *Catch-22*, it was the elegance of the photograph that mattered, not hitting the target.

Like the top officers in *Catch-22*, the leading thinkers in the financial industry have long used the elegance of statistics — specifically, standard deviation or "volatility" — to frame the definition of risk. It sounds so simple: The greater the standard deviation of returns, the greater the volatility; and, the greater the volatility, the greater the risk. It worked so cleanly on the blackboards of academia it just had to be used in the boardrooms of America. There was only one problem.

The theory was wrong.

To paraphrase my favorite physicist, Richard Feynman, "A guess that is wrong is wrong, no matter how elegant, no matter who made it."

If the old paradigm of risk is dead, what new paradigm has replaced it? I can't fully answer this question until Section V of this book. In the meantime, it would help you understand the eventual answer if I explained first why these great minds of finance let their Over-Confidence get the better of them.

They say a picture is worth a thousand words. With apologies to Joseph Heller, I'll show you exactly what's wrong with volatility as a measure of risk by using his example of dysfunction in the following illustration:

Illustration 1. – The Catch 22 of Volatility

Source: Author

Illustration 1 shows us an example of a "tight bombing pattern," another way of saying "low volatility." See how the five explosions in the Mediterranean Sea are all very close to the straight dotted line. That's the kind of picture that would make General Peckem giddy and earn Plane A's flight crew a medal.

Now look at the much larger spread of the bombing pattern for Plane B. Man, those explosions are all over the place. This is another way of saying "high volatility." Despite hitting the smack-dab middle of the target, this flight crew, in Joseph Heller's *Catch-22* world, isn't getting a medal. No, it's probably being sent to some sort of sensitivity training class, if not another mission.

This simple illustration explains the how and why standard deviation fell from its exalted heights. If you'd like the real explanation — warning, it uses some statistical terminology — then you should read *Appendix IV: Volatility as Risk – Where it All Began and Why it Went Wrong*.

Many purveyors of financial advice have long recognized the fiasco of defining risk in terms of volatility. "Volatility as a description of risk is inadequate for many reasons," says Matthew B. Boersen, Partner at Straight Path Wealth Management in Grand Rapids, Michigan. In a nod to Markowitz's original concerns, he says, "First, volatility by its definition describes both upside movements and downside movements. Theoretically, a stock or fund could have a high volatility measure for a one-year period, while never dropping below the original 52-week low. Because advisors use volatility to describe risk, participants equate volatility with negativity, even if it measures both positive and negative movements."

"Volatility fails two-fold," says Kevin Conard, Co-Founder of Blooom.com in Overland Park, Kansas. "For starters it has a negative connotation. When an investor hears the term 'volatility,' he instantly assumes it is a dangerous scary roller-coaster-ride of an investment. When in fact, volatility is a 401k saver's best friend, allowing him to dollar cost average into positions in his account. Secondly, volatility fails to frame risk correctly. Risk should be defined as the failure to build up a 401k/retirement account that will sustain an independent retirement that out-paces inflation — that is true risk."

Jamie Hopkins, Esq., Assistant Professor of Taxation in the Retirement Income Program at The American College in Bryn Mawr, Pennsylvania, and Associate Director of the New York Life Center for Retirement Income, says, "Volatility fails as a real-world definition of risk for the regular investor because it is too narrow. Volatility shows us one level of risk but does not explain all of the concerns and threats to the investor. For example, a product might have low volatility but no liquidity. This represents a risk to the investor that does not show up in the definition of risk when defined by volatility."

Perhaps the greatest sin of volatility was its failure to act as advertised in the two recent market crises. Joe Gordon, Managing Partner at Gordon Asset Management, LLC, in Raleigh-Durham/Chapel Hill, North Carolina, says, "You can back test all you want but we tell them to go back to 2000-2002, and 2008/09, and recall how poorly equities performed. When bad things happen, as in 2008/09, most all correlations approached one. In other words, volatility told you nothing because everything performed poorly."

Boersen says, "Volatility measures have a bad track record of guiding investments and understanding true risk. For instance, volatility measures were at all-time highs in March of 2009, scaring many participants into pulling money out of the market at exactly the wrong moment. I actually have a client whom I met in 2011, and when reviewing his 401k statements, we discovered he had called in an investment change from equity funds to cash in his 401k on March 9, 2009 — the day the market bottomed!" In other words, making a decision based on the volatility at the time turned out to be the worst decision possible.

Since the rise of behavioral economics over the last dozen years or so, many in the academic world, especially younger researchers, see MPT and, especially, the use of standard deviation or volatility to define risk, as well past their expiration dates. Yet, you can still find references to MPT in the marketing literature of most major investment firms. In fact, two of the top ERISA attorneys in the country — Marcia Wagner and Fred Reish — both told me the DOL considers MPT a "generally accepted investment theory." This makes it very difficult — if not a breach of their fiduciary duty — for 401k plan sponsors to omit MPT from their investment due diligence.

"The financial services industry has for far too long held onto the traditional academic definition of volatility and risk when talking to clients about their investments and portfolios," says Hopkins. "While these definitions have their place, it is often not in discussions with clients. Instead, the industry needs to continue to separate risk from volatility as the only measurement stick. Instead, risk should be viewed as the threat to future unwanted events or changes. In some areas, the industry drives academia and in others, academia drives the industry. Unfortunately, the traditional definition of academic portfolio risk is out of date and does not accurately represent client concerns."

Although most modern academics generally recognize volatility as an inappropriate proxy for risk, industry professionals continue to stand by it, even if their endorsements often include significant qualifications. For example, Katie Stokes, Director of Financial Planning at J.E. Wilson Advisors, LLC in Columbia, South Carolina, believes "Defining 'risk' as volatility is not inherently incorrect, it just isn't very helpful to the average (or even above average) investor. So much focus is placed on volatility because the impact can be great when not handled correctly."

When will investment firms catch up to current academic theory? "Unfortunately the industry is slow to change. I think it's a term that has become part of the common vernacular and no one has challenged or identified what true risk is for an investor who might live 30 years into retirement," says Conard.

That MPT remained unchallenged for almost two generations and because it had been born from such mathematical rigor makes it hard to replace. Anthony Alfidi, CEO of Alfidi Capital in San Francisco, California, says, "The academic definition of volatility has lasted so long because there is no widely accepted replacement that carries a similar statistical validation. Stochastic (a fancy way of saying 'statistics-based' alternatives are [only now] beginning to receive validation in academic research."

Some in the financial community are not so charitable. The fact is MPT techniques have been incorporated quite successfully in sales literature over the decades. Some see the industry as reluctant to give up such an effective sales tool just because it doesn't work as advertised. Leonard P. Raskin, of AEP Raskin Global in Hunt Valley, Maryland, says, "I believe the industry doesn't care what the investor knows or doesn't know. They simply want to accumulate as much money under management as possible to maximize fund company fees."

Joseph Carbone, Jr, Wealth Advisor and Partner at Focus Planning Group in Bayport, New York, says, "I think it's one of the things in our industry that is not always developed or marketed with the novice investor in mind. Many times our industry and advisors do not understand what the retail public really wants."

Matthew Grishman, Co-Founder of 401kMasters, a subsidiary of Gebhardt Group, Inc. in Lafayette, California, says, "We believe the industry has held onto its beliefs about volatility for its own self-interest, and that interest is for the benefit of collecting fees. The industry has promoted a 'buy and hold' strategy as the only way to manage volatility for this very purpose. They have leveraged the 24-hour media cycle as a way to keep volatility in front of millions of investors to promote their fee-collecting agenda. 'Stay invested through volatility because you don't want to miss the best days of performance.' Although we agree buy and hold has worked for investors sometimes — during two extended bull markets (post WWII and 1982-2000) — it was also the cause for so many investors to lose 30-60% of their life savings in 2008-2009. Despite investor losses, the industry kept promoting buy and hold so investors remained invested, allowing the industry to continue collecting fees."

Ironically, it may be that inertia alone keeps this ball rolling. And that inertia comes in the form of your friendly neighborhood compliance department. If ever there were a need to exemplify "herd mentality," compliance would fill that bill quickly. It's tough to say "no" to a Nobel Prize-winning concept. It's just as difficult to say "yes" to the latest that finance professors have to offer. Boersen says, "I think compliance concerns have driven the over-utilization of substituting volatility for risk. Whether it be a plan custodian putting together education literature, or an advisor putting together an education presentation, compliance restrictions many times limit the usefulness of adequately describing risk and volatility. Because of this, advisors often have two choices for words when talking about investment downsides, either 'risk' or 'volatility,' as most compliance departments accept those terms."

Travis Freeman, President of Four Seasons Financial Education in St. Louis, Missouri, says, "The industry as a whole cannot grasp a more consumer-friendly definition of volatility due to legal reasons. For example, one may explain the negatives of volatility as the risk of losing money. However, that doesn't register with most people. What does register is providing a hard number, such as a dollar amount. For example, explaining volatility and standard deviation as 'a 67% chance of losing or gaining as much as $50,000' makes much more sense to the layperson. However, I cannot imagine any compliance department in the United States allowing this to go to print."

The use of terms like "volatility" or "standard deviation," even if used properly, fail to connect with the typical investor. Conard says, "Most investors define risk as the loss of their portfolio. We reframe the problem. We help them understand that showing up at their retirement party without enough assets to sustain an independent retirement is the true risk."

In addition, risk comes in many flavors, not the one implied by a single statistical number called volatility. Hopkins says, "When talking to investors about risk, specific risks need to be addressed instead of talking about just portfolio volatility risk. For example, liquidity, loss of spouse, sequence of return, and public policy risk all need to be addressed. As such, it is important to rank and gauge the investor's risks. If the loss of one spouse due to an early death would require significant withdrawals from the portfolio, this risk needs to be understood and addressed to minimize potential losses. Lastly, it is crucial to make sure clients know that when you deal with one level of risk, you often exacerbate another area of risk. As such, in the real world investors need to be comfortable with some level of risk, whether it is volatility, inflation, or liquidity."

Robert C. Lawton, President at Lawton Retirement Plan Consultants in Milwaukee, Wisconsin, says, "Volatility is one aspect of risk. There are many others. Political, legislative, currency, economic, corporate, industry, and other risks might be more important to consider, depending upon the investment. Investors who characterize risk in terms of volatility only may be missing the larger picture."

"The definition of risk is too narrowly defined by volatility," says Dan Dingus, President and Chief Operating Officer at Fragasso Financial Advisors in Pittsburgh, Pennsylvania.

Unfortunately, advisers cannot recap a long list of risks to most investors. The vast array of risks will tend to bewilder investors in much the same way a seven page dinner menu stuns diners. Investors demand the simplicity of a single number, a simplicity once provided by using standard deviation to measure risk. Maybe, though, the answer doesn't lie in the risk part of the risk-return relationship. Maybe the answer can only be found in the other half of the equation that started this whole movement.

Before we get to that, we need to go over one more thing: You. Specifically, the power you have at your disposal. Remember what I said at the beginning of this book. (I know you'll pass the 100-page mark before you hit the next chapter, but the book isn't so long that you should have forgotten what I wrote about earlier: you being in control of your own destiny.) When it comes to successful retirement saving, not only is it possible, but, as the pioneers before you have shown, it's also really easy to achieve. The next section shows you how incredibly easy it is. Plus, for those of you with children, there's a special bonus you just won't believe.

SECTION FOUR:

– THE POWER OF YOU –

THREE CRITICAL COMPONENTS TO RETIREMENT SUCCESS (AND WHY "4" IS THE MAGIC NUMBER)

CHAPTER TWENTY:
STUDY REVEALS THREE 401K STRATEGIES
MORE IMPORTANT THAN YOUR
INVESTMENT SELECTION

I like Galileo. He's one of my historical heroes. It's not because he was Italian. It's not because he was an astronomer. It's not because he accomplished his greatest feat as a septuagenarian. These were all fine attributes, but the thing that I really like about Galileo was his nickname. He got it when he was in school and it stuck with him his entire life. They called him "The Wrangler."

No, Galileo was not a cowboy. And he wasn't merely a trouble-maker (although his "wranglerness" did make trouble). He was, however, an independent thinker unafraid to take on the establishment.

Can you see why I like him so much?

He wasn't afraid to take on the powers-that-be no matter what the consequences. And he did. And there were consequences.

I'm reminded of that every time I start a discussion involving the term "asset allocation" (and, to a lesser extent, Modern Portfolio Theory). You see, the financial services industry has invested a great deal in these concepts and they don't take it too lightly when anyone questions their premises. But, as with Galileo, I'm a trained scientist. All scientists are taught to constantly question and test prevailing theory. The best scientists disregard political correctness, frame these questions in the language of the mass market, then go over the heads of the authority to ask these questions directly to the public.

This represents the greatness of Galileo and, incidentally, of Richard Feynman, another science hero of mine. "Why not Einstein?" you ask. Einstein was a one-of-a-kind genius. I'm just a regular guy. Galileo and Feynman were regular guys. Galileo used the vernacular language of his time (Italian) rather than the haughty language of science (Latin) when he wrote. Why? He wrote so everybody could understand. In a similar vein, Feynman could effortlessly take the most complex concepts of quantum physics and reduce them to the easy-to-understand language of regular people.

That's my goal, only my subject area is finance, not physics.

As we saw with Galileo, there's a risk in questioning authority. (Feynman was lucky to have lived in a time when "question authority" was, ironically, the ethos of the establishment. That being said, he still found ways to tweak the self-important crowd.) In either case, the risk lies not just in upsetting the applecart, but in apathy, intellectual bigotry, and blacklisting.

When a scientist or industry expert takes his case to the masses, usually the public ignores them. Often the public merely thinks he's just another example of zany egg-headedness. But sometimes the public will listen to him and understand. A collective light bulb goes off and the path to true change is forged.

The establishment, on the other hand, immediately vilifies these mavericks. I know. This happened to me. But that's a tale for another time.

Have you ever found yourself in a similar situation? Believe me, it's in this antiestablishment spirit that I want you to absorb this chapter. Be warned, there are those who may fervently disagree with the conclusions, but the numbers don't lie. This is the beauty (some would call it a curse) of science. The only faith required is a faith in mathematics. All else is fiddle faddle. Don't fiddle faddle.

For nearly 20 years, financial service providers have claimed the secret to retirement success lies in "asset allocation," or, in words normal people use, "investment selection." Both professional and academic careers have been made on this premise. A 2012 study, however, offers an alarming assessment of the fruits of over-emphasizing investment selection — and has the real-life numbers to back up its conclusions. (Wait. Haven't we seen this word "over" before?) Additionally, this study also suggests the current debate surrounding a popular but controversial 401k product may amount to nothing more than arguing how many angels can dance on the head of a pin. (Arguing how many angels can dance on the head of a pin was said to have been a favorite pastime among medieval theologians. It made for great entertainment, but it really had nothing to do with the matter at hand.)

In "How Important Is Asset Allocation To Americans' Financial Retirement Security?" (*Pension Research Council Working Paper*, The Wharton School, University of Pennsylvania, August, 2012), authors Alicia H. Munnell, Natalia Orlova, and Anthony Webb, using real-world data, may have turned the 401k world upside down. By analyzing data from the RETIRE project at Georgia State University, the Social

Security Administration, and the Health and Retirement Study, these researchers concluded that investment selection has a much smaller impact on success in attaining retirement goals than popular opinion — and many marketing programs of large financial service firms — would have us believe. Indeed, they identified three factors that can influence retirement outcomes more favorably — and with far greater control and predictability — for employees.

Most experienced financial planners and investment advisers may already be familiar with at least two of these three "levers," as the paper calls them. Astute 401k plan sponsors, who focus more on employee education than the plan's investment menu, may also recognize these levers. It's high time that you, the individual 401k saver, know what these three levers are. Why? Because they all involve you and you can have full control over each and every one of them. Like I said, the power is you.

The three behavioral strategies shown in the paper to be more important than asset allocation are: Controlling spending (i.e., investing early); Delaying retirement; and Taking out a reverse mortgage (which is probably less relevant to the typical reader of this book). At least that's what the paper's language said. If you're a typical person who doesn't spend his or her idle time investigating financial research theses, allow me to re-interpret these three levers in a language practical to 401k investors. The three critical components to earning enough money to retire comfortably are:

1) When You Start Saving,
2) How Much You Contribute; and,
3) When You Retire.

Remember those three factors. They represent the greatest lesson you can learn from this book. They are your destiny. You control all three components. You control your destiny.

Unfortunately, even with the benefit of this knowledge, retirement savers tend to ignore its true meaning. I spoke with Anthony Webb, a senior economist at the Center for Retirement Research who holds a Ph.D. in economics from the University of California, San Diego and is one of the paper's authors. He told me, "I am sure that, when drawing up a financial plan, reputable financial advisors would ensure that the savings rate and planned retirement age are consistent with the planned retirement age. Many online tools illustrate the impact of early retirement, but few households avail themselves of such advice."

The authors' use of practical financial and return targets rather than historic market returns differentiates this paper from others like it. This "goal-oriented targeting" approach (which I'll discuss more thoroughly in the next section of the book) more closely mimics the factors and decisions retirement savers need to consider. As a result, the paper concludes "starting to save at age 25, rather than age 45, cuts the required savings rate by about two-thirds." Similarly, it says "delaying retirement from age 62 to age 70 also reduces the required savings rate by about two-thirds." Just how dramatic is the impact of saving early and retiring later? The paper shows someone who begins saving at age 25 and retires at age 70 need only save 7% of his income. Contrast that to the individual who begins saving at age 45 and wishes to retire at age 62. That person will need to save an unrealistic 65% of his salary. On the other hand, that same "late" 45-year old saver would "only" have to defer 18% of his annual salary if he delayed retirement until age 70. This illustrates the power of all three levers you control — the "When You Start Saving" lever; the "How to Make Up for a Late Start by Increasing Your Annual Contribution" (a.k.a. "How Much You Contribute") lever; and the "How to Make Up for a Late Start by Working Longer" (a.k.a. "When You Retire") lever. It also shows that second lever is less reliable than either the first or the third levers.

The above results assume a rate of return of 4%, but this is less than half the historical long-term return of stocks. With this in mind, the authors also looked at varying the annual return rate because, as we all know, higher returns allow for smaller annual savings deferral rates. This is where the first surprise came. The study showed that a wide (for the typical multi-decade period associated with retirement investing) swing in annual returns can easily be made up for by deferring retirement. The paper concludes "an individual can offset the impact of a 2% return instead of a 6% return by retiring at 67 instead of 62." Again, this is one of the levers you control — the "When You Retire" lever.

"The papers' findings are actually quite hopeful," says Webb. "While recognizing that ill health or unemployment will prevent a minority of older households from delaying retirement, the message is that the remainder have a powerful lever at their disposal to get back on track."

When you start saving, how much you contribute, and when you retire. That's all you need to know. That's all you need to act on. Everything else is just window dressing.

And what about the one thing everyone is always talking about – investments? Well, let's go back to the study to find our answer.

The paper addresses this by getting into the nitty-gritty of investment selection, or, to use the term the authors use, "asset allocation." It looks at typical wage earners and high wage earners and compares retirement outcomes using two different asset allocations — a "typical" and an "optimal" asset allocation. This is where we discover the second shocking conclusion. The difference in real-life impact between a "typical" and an "optimal" asset allocation is merely a few months' salary. In other words, working an additional few months makes up for any ground lost as a result of using a sub-optimal asset allocation. Specifically, the paper says, "The cost of retaining a typical portfolio (57% in equities), rather than switching to an optimal portfolio (100% in equities), is… just over four months' salary." The study concludes, "In short, regardless of the degree of risk aversion, asset allocation is relatively unimportant for the typical household."

"We are not suggesting asset allocation be totally disregarded, only that getting it right will have only a modest impact on retirement outcomes for most households," says Webb. He adds, "It is certainly not something to be ignored. Households need all the help they can get. But it has a second order effect, relative to working longer. Our research shows that the great majority of households (70+%) will be able to maintain their pre-retirement standard of living if they delay retirement till age 70."

Webb also told me the results of the paper may hint to HR implications for plan sponsors. He says, "Given the amounts most households have accumulated in their 401k plans, few will be able to maintain their pre-retirement standard of living in retirement. Many of those who are able to, will likely choose to delay retirement. Plan sponsors need to ensure they are able to make productive use of these workers."

He also points out the folly of the current "to" or "through" glide debate regarding target date funds. (This debates argues whether the "date" in the target date fund refers to the date you retire (the "to") or the date you intend to begin taking distributions after you retire (the "through"). Webb says, "Which target date fund you choose matters less than the other three levers." Plan sponsors and employees confused and concerned about the target date fund controversy might be relieved to hear that. Large mutual fund companies counting on target date funds to help them accumulate more assets and increase revenues might be a bit disappointed by this new reality.

When you start investing, how much you contribute, and when you retire. Remember those three components. They have the greatest impact on your ability to live a successful retirement. And you control all of them. Asset allocation — or investing — is a fourth component, but you can't control it and it's really not as important as the other three.

You control these three levers. Nobody can stop you from using them. They are in your hands. You are free to do with them what you want. They can guarantee a successful retirement. You control them. You — and you alone — have the power to guarantee yourself a successful retirement. No one can take it away from you.

Got it?

Now, let's take a look at each of the levers. I'll give you some better examples than these researchers gave. These examples are so easy to understand, you can (and should) show them to your children. I know. When I give this part of the presentation to various groups, they invariably ask, "Chris, do you have something about this that I can give to my kids?" What is it they're asking for? It's the same thing we're all asking for. It's...

CHAPTER TWENTY-ONE: HOW TO RETIRE A MILLIONAIRE (HINT: IT'S EASIER THAN YOU THINK)

L ike other fathers and mothers today, I've had the honor to serve as a Scout Leader. In a way, it allowed me to ride shotgun with my son as he progressed from a wide-eyed Tiger Cub, to a crafty Cub Scout, to an outdoorsman Boy Scout and, finally, through to the hands-on project management-oriented (and, yes, honorable) Eagle Scout he is today. Among the many fun things I've done was counseling boys on their merit badges. My favorites were Astronomy, Journalism, and Robotics, but the kids mostly came to me for Personal Management. That's the one that had to do with money and finances. For some reason, they figured I knew something about that. Maybe it had to do with being introduced as a "registered investment adviser."

There's something about being introduced as an investment adviser that leads people to generalizations. One of the most frequent questions I get from non-financial people who have just met me is, "How can I become a millionaire?" I usually laugh, hoping the person isn't serious, and turn the discussion to something eminently more fascinating like what an analysis of ultraviolent radiation patterns in horizontal branch stars can tell us about stellar evolution. (Yes, I really know what that means, and, yes, there's a reason why I'm such a wallflower at "networking" events.)

Nonetheless, I happened to stumble upon the answer to this age-old question while counseling a group of Boy Scouts for their Personal Management merit badge. The answer was so obvious — and so easy — that I have since worked it into almost every 401k employee education program I do. To discover the answer, I'll refer back to the study I wrote about in the last chapter.

The study discussed the four factors that lead to retirement success (defined as "saving enough to retire in comfort"). Do you remember what they are? If you don't, go back and re-read the chapter. OK, I'll be nice (this time) and first reiterate the Four Steps to Retirement Success: 1) Understand the basics of retirement success; 2) Avoid the Common Mistakes of Retirement Savers; 3) Emphasize the Three Critical Components to Retirement Success; and, 4) Create, Implement, and Monitor a Personal Plan. Going back to that third item for a moment, do you also remember which three of these four factors you control? I'll be very disappointed with you if you don't.

Of the three you control, one is most critical and easiest to achieve.

This chapter is about that most significant component to retirement success.

Are you ready? Here it is: Invest Early. [Author's Note: Don't worry if you think you're "too old" for "early." I'll show you the options you have after we get through this part.]

That's it. No more. No less. It's also so overused that it has become a cliché. The trick, then, is to use an incredibly shocking example — so shocking it will open your eyes in multiple dimensions. That's where the Boy Scout merit badge comes in.

You see, I can think of no other group less interested in retirement than your typical Boy Scout. Whether it's girls, sports, robotics, video games, or just about any other activity involving either building something or destroying something, each of these far outrank "retirement readiness" on the teenage thought meter. Still, if they wanted to earn the merit badge, they had to "get it." Since no valid educational theory involves the use of a sledgehammer, I had to rely on the next best things. These are the things adolescent boys seem to respond to the most: graphics, silliness, and becoming a millionaire.

Come to think of it, experience proves it's not just adolescent boys who seem to respond to these three things.

Anyway, I tell the boys about the story of two friends: Early Earl and Late Larry. As suggested, Earl tended to do things early. He'd finish his homework before he got home from school. This allowed him to play and the watch TV without any worry. Larry, on the other hand, usually put things off until the last possible minute. He'd be still doing his homework the morning before school and find, instead of watching his favorite NFL team lose to the Buffalo Bills on Sunday, he'd be stuck in his room working on school work that had been assigned days before.

Both boys were able to find jobs when they were fifteen and would work — even during their college years — until they retired at age 70. But when they retired, Early Earl found he could live much more comfortably than Late Larry.

Why?

Because Earl invested early. In fact, Earl began saving for his retirement when he started working at age 15. He opened up an IRA.

Now, he didn't earn too much in those early years and especially through college, so he only saved $1,000 a year until he turned 30. Then he stopped saving. We don't know why. Maybe he bought a bigger house and had to pay a big mortgage. Maybe he started saving for his own children's college education. Maybe, if he was really smart, he started his own child modeling agency, hired his children as infants and put money into his kids' retirement accounts from before they even started to crawl. (Why would I use such an odd example?)

Hmm, let's not get ahead of ourselves.

So there's Early Earl at age 31, having saved a grand total of $16,000. What's Late Larry been up to? Well, he's been, uh, late. He hasn't saved anything for his retirement. He's figuring that he'll earn more when he's older, so he can save more then. And he does. For sixteen years beginning age 40, Late Larry saves $5,000 a year. That's five times more than Early Earl. In fact, by the time he's done saving at age 55, Late Larry has saved $80,000.

Late Larry has contributed five times more to his retirement than Early Earl. Can you guess which one has more money when they each retire at the ripe-old age of 70? As the graph below shows, by investing even a small amount earlier, Earl is able to grow his assets to $711,483 when he retires. Late Larry, though, with so much less time to grow, retires with only $519,446 — even though he saved five times more than Early Earl! (The growth assumption is 8% annually — a long-term rate you'd typically find in an all-equity mutual fund.)

Graph 8. The Power of Investing Early

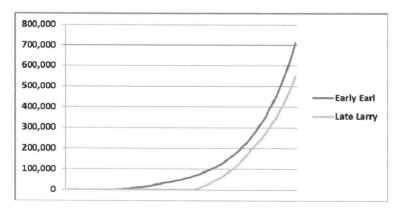

Source: Author

Incidentally, if Early Earl wanted to have a million dollars when he retires at age 70, instead of saving $1,000 a year for sixteen years, he'd only have to increase that number to $1,406 a year for sixteen years. This would equal a total savings of only $22,496 – still substantially less than Late Larry's total contribution of $80,000.

Why does Early Earl have a seemingly insurmountable advantage over Late Larry? For those familiar with the term, this graph shows the "Time Value of Money." Mark Donnelly, Portfolio Manager at AEPG(r) Wealth Strategies in Warren, New Jersey, says, "The power of compounding returns is more and more valuable the longer the timeframe. Saving just a little at a young age can have a far greater impact than much larger amounts further down the road because of this."

Elle Kaplan, says, "The key to retirement saving success is to save consistently and to start early. The beauty of investing is that time is on your side: the longer that your wealth is invested in the markets where it can grow, the more potential impact your savings can have. If you start investing when you are a teenager, you will have nearly five decades of growth before you turn 65. Essentially, your money works for you."

"This is the power of compound interest," explains Matthew Moore, Founder of Clear Retirement Group in Portland, Oregon. "The teenager has contributed $16,000 dollars in total of his own money but has given himself 20+ years for it to earn interest before the 40 year old even starts saving money. My family ran into this very same problem and didn't start saving money for retirement until they were in their early 40s. Unfortunately for them, they are now playing catch up and throwing as much of their extra income at their retirement accounts as they can." Of course, what are the odds of a teenager — or even most adults — understanding the concept of "compound interest"?

Remember the importance of silliness. Sometimes silliness comes in funny names (think "Early Earl" and "Late Larry") and sometimes it comes in funny visualizations. Howard Pressman, Financial Planner at Egan, Berger and Weiner, LLC in Vienna, Virginia, uses a funny visualization to explain compounding, a term often difficult for teenagers (and even their parents) to comprehend. He says, "Remember the cartoon of the little snowball that starts at the top of the hill and gets bigger and bigger and bigger as it rolls downhill, and then eventually it gets so big it wipes out the town? That's compounding. You are earning interest on the interest that you earned in prior periods. Just like the farther the snowball rolls the larger it gets, the longer your money has to grow, the larger it gets too. This is one of the most powerful forces in all of finance."

Of course, you already know that. But do your kids? (Likely "no.") Does it matter? (Definitely "yes.") What can be done about it? Let's take a break from talking about you and learn how the best way to help yourself is by helping someone else. The next chapter shows what I mean.

Chapter Twenty-Two:
Here's the Best Way to Learn the Lesson

Why don't we see a lot of "teenage" millionaires? First, IRAs haven't been around long enough for our hypothetical 15 year old to have reached 70 yet. More to the point, though, is why we haven't seen a lot of teenage IRAs in the first place. "In my experience of dealing with young savers," says Michael Lecours, Financial Advisor & Marketing Manager at Ohanesian/Lecours in West Hartford, Connecticut, "they will always have a reason not to invest — not enough money, simply forgot, or need money to pay other expenses. Something comes along that seems to be more important than saving for something that won't be used for 50 years."

Matthew Moore says, "For teenagers, retirement is so far away. There are so many things for which money would provide more instant gratification, such as a new car, new clothes, or eating out. Saving for retirement at that age is not what kids think about nor is it what gets positively reinforced by their peers."

"It's hard for teenagers to save for retirement because they can't comprehend retirement," says Howard Pressman. "It is so far into the future that it is not even remotely a part of their frame of reference. It's hard to get many adults to save for retirement and they're closer. Retirement is for old people, they're young and they think they'll be that way forever. I know I'm constantly surprised when I look in the mirror."

"When you are a teenager you aren't thinking about retirement, you are thinking about taking a girl to the movies or buying the newest video game or pair of shoes," says Brett Gottlieb, an advisor at Comprehensive Advisor in Carlsbad, California. "With so many distractions and marketing messages being sent their way, it's impossible to think about the future, it's about the now. What's the hottest thing out? what will my friends say if I get this cool jacket or game? These are what matter at that age, so it's not about changing the mindset of a teen at that age, it's about teaching them a value from a different angle."

"Financial education should start at an early age preaching that the sooner you start saving, the more you could have to spend later," says

Dan Dingus. "Without proper financial education, they have no context to relate passing on the latte or the additional fast food meal versus savings for retirement which appears so distant. But in fact as mentioned, the value of compounding is so powerful at an early age. It is not how much you save but for how long."

The idea of parents or grandparents saving for their children/grandchildren — whether through traditional tax savings or specialty trusts — is not new. John Graves, Managing Principal of a mid-sized RIA in Ventura, California, has "clients who are saving for their teenage grandchildren."

"The select few clients and children I know who have learned about savings and stuck with it over time have always been connected to parents or grandparents who were good savers and started them off on the right foot, teaching them how to set goals for themselves and how to achieve those goals through calculated steps," says Gottlieb. "I have had clients bring their kids to appointments when they were in their teens and had them learn about investing and the types of concepts and planning I do with their parents. I think all parents should include their children in the planning process to some extent; it will teach them about the importance of saving. Specifically, most clients have had the children open a checking account and place birthday and holiday gifts into these accounts so they can see them through online statements. Many have shown them their 529 college savings accounts and explained how those accounts got started and have grown."

But using a retirement vehicle like an IRA is quite rare. What's the best way to get a teenager to start an IRA? Donnelly says, "From my experience learning to save and maintaining that level of discipline over time is a skill handed down from attentive parents. Either it is as simple as 'do as I do' and following their parents methods (with a little guidance), to a full-fledged reward system that encourages both work and savings by matching portions of a teenager's savings. Either way can work, but the former puts more of the burden of self-motivation on the part of the teenager."

Anthony VanDyke, President of ALV Mortgage in Salt Lake City, Utah, is an example of someone who started saving in an IRA as a teenager. "I started saving for retirement as a teenager," says VanDyke. "The reason I started saving early is because of something my high school math teacher once told me: 'There are two types of people in this world: Those who pay interest and those who earn interest.'" Still,

VanDyke believes it's primarily the parents' duty to lead by example. "I think it is hard for teenagers to save for retirement because they do not see their parents saving for retirement. Over 80% of my mortgage customers have no retirement savings. Either they have never saved or they wiped it out over the last few years during the financial crisis."

"There are always those teens who were raised to be savers and those that will always be spenders," says Moore. "We all know someone who worked two or three jobs over the summer to pay for a new car. Or maybe those who saved all through high school to pay their way through college. Some people are taught these personal finance techniques and others aren't. But to focus on retirement in their teens, that is a special breed. In my work as a financial advisor to corporate retirement plans I did come across the 18 and 19 year old employee who was actively contributing to a 401k plan. They knew by putting away a set percentage or dollar amount every pay period, pre-tax, that they would be systematically contributing to their financial well-being.

And for those of you wondering if it makes sense for college-bound teenagers to start saving for retirement, Pressman says, "Retirement accounts are not counted on the Free Application for Federal Student Aid (FAFSA) because withdrawing from 401ks or traditional IRAs would typically create an early withdrawal penalty."

Adds Moore: "A qualified retirement account such as a 401k or IRA, whether owned by the parent or by the child, is not counted when determining financial aid. I believe it to be a good idea so that more students and families don't resort to retirement assets to pay for college. If these assets are not included in the financial aid calculation they will receive more help for education and not have to dip into their retirement savings."

"Neither students nor parents are required to report qualified retirement assets (regular or Roth IRAs, 401k plans, etc.) on the FAFSA," says Gottlieb. "So when it comes to determining aid eligibility, these assets don't count. (Please note: If your child took a distribution from an IRA, that would be considered income, would be reported on the FAFSA, and would affect eligibility — but that's a very unlikely scenario.) These being exempt are a good idea and allow for you to begin saving at an even younger age than many would think was even possible for retirement savings."

"The challenge," says Ozeme Bonnette, "is that contributions must be reported, so it's better to do it early on than in the year or years right before completing the FAFSAs."

Everyone speaks to the challenges of educating employees when it comes to financial literacy and their retirement plan. But do you know the best way to learn? The best way to learn is by teaching. And that's the lesson to take away from this example. Whenever I use the "Boy Scout" example in front of a group of 401k plan participants, I invariably get the question, "Hey! Can you put this into something I can show my kid?" I almost always answer, "Go ahead and use what I showed you and explain it yourself." I know that if they're willing to explain it to their own children, then they "get it." And that, Charlie Brown, is what education is all about.

While he acknowledges teenagers "use the money to chase girls and buy clothes, (has anything changed?)" Dean R. Hedeker, of Hedeker Wealth Management in Chicago, Illinois, perhaps best gets to the heart of the matter when he says, "The best thing is that they get a job and then take their earnings and put it in an IRA. The kids will be millionaires by 65."

You think this is good? There's actually an idea I floated in several of my articles that takes this premise to the Xtreme. (Kids are attracted to doing things in the Xtreme. Kids are also attracted to spelling "extreme" by taking the initial "e" out and capitalizing the "x": "Xtreme." I know all this because ESPN told me.) It was so compelling I worked it into my standard presentations.

Interested? Check out *Appendix V The Child IRA — Solution to the Coming Social Security Crisis?*

In the meantime, let's not forget the lesson of Early Earl and Late Larry. Maybe there's hope for Larry after all. Maybe you'll find out in the next chapter. (OK, I'll quit teasing. You will find out how Late Larry can catch up in the next chapter.)

Chapter Twenty-Three:
Late Larry's Reprieve –
What's Holding You Back?

O K, I lied. First I'll show what gave me the idea of *Appendix V*. In updating the chart for Early Earl and Late Larry, I accidentally started Early Earl at Age 0 (i.e., as a newborn). This caused me to add a new character — Turbo Tot. If you weren't convinced about the value of investing early after the last two chapters, Turbo Tot will turn you around. Check out this graph:

Graph 9. Turbo Tot Saves America

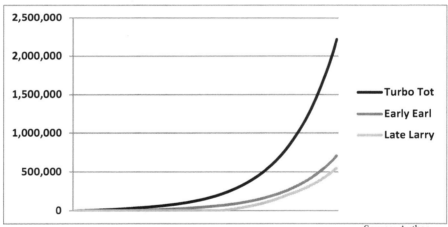

Source: Author

Recall last time that Early Earl invested $1,000 a year from ages 15 through 30 and reaped $711,483 when he retired at age 70. Likewise, Late Larry invested $5,000 a year from ages 40 through 55 and ended up with $519,446 by age 70. What did Turbo Tot do to far surpass the other two? Turbo Tot invested $1,000 annually from the day he was born through his eighteenth birthday. That gave him $2,212,644 by the time he turned 70. If you want to know why Turbo Tot Saves America, then read *Appendix V*. (Growth in all these examples is the same 8% per year we've been using.)

The initial point here is again why it's so important to start investing early. Late Larry gave Early Earl a 25-year head start and still ended up with about three-quarters of what Early Earl ended up with. Turbo Tot, on the hand, only had a 15-year head start on Early Earl yet ended up with three times as much as Early Earl.

Wow. No wonder why everyone says Einstein said compounding is the most powerful force in the universe.

This chapter, though, isn't about investing early. That's the first lever (or first gear if you remember our muscle car analogy). Here, we want to focus on the second level — your level of contributions. If you're behind where you should be, then increasing your contribution level might just be what the doctor ordered. The IRS caught on to this idea several years ago and began allowing those aged 50 and over a chance to "catch-up." This "Catch-Up" provision allows (as of this writing) people in this age group to contribute anywhere from $1,000 to $6,500 above the normal contribution limit. Let's take a look at how this works using the above graph. And, just because he's such a nice guy, we'll continue to pick on Late Larry as an example.

For the sake of argument, let's assume Late Larry only invests from age 40 through age 55. At his current rate, he's a shade below Early Earl. All is not lost for Late Larry, though, for he can apply his second lever and increase his contribution rate in order to match Early Earl. To end up with $711,581 at age 70, Late Larry can up his annual contribution from day one to $6,469 (from $5,000). This may be a very doable alternative for Late Larry.

Things don't look so good for catching up to Turbo Tot. Larry would need to increase his annual contribution to $20,115. This is a very high number and, in most cases (at least as of the writing of this book) well beyond the maximum allowable contribution for most people in most retirement plans. In short, Late Larry doesn't have a reasonable chance to catch up to Turbo Tot.

The same is not necessarily true for Early Earl. He would need to save $2,110 more than the $1,000 he's putting away. That's a total of $3,110 per year. It sounds doable, but remember, Early Earl is starting out at age 15, and $3,000 is a lot of money for a 15 year old.

Now, so far we've only been speaking about absolute dollar numbers. That's one way to invest and, as we'll see in Section V of this book, speaking in terms of absolute dollars is the only way to set your retirement goal. The industry uses a different nomenclature to describe contributions. They call contributions "deferrals." What? Did you just ask "What does 'nomenclature' mean?" It's a fancy way of saying "name." Just like "deferral" is a fancy way of saying "contribution." Don't ask me why the industry chose the harder word. Just keep in mind, if you're sitting in a 401k education meeting and someone says the word "deferral," understand they are talking about contributions. Worse, the industry describes deferrals in terms of percentages, not in terms of those absolute dollars you actually pay out every month.

Since it's described in terms of a percentage, the beauty of a word like "deferral," though, is it allows the ability to compare savings rates rather quickly. Coincidentally, the company match is usually also spoken of in terms of a percent. Often, you'll hear something like "a company will match dollar-for-dollar up to the first 3% of your salary." That's when using the deferral rate rather than the absolute dollars of the contribution makes the most sense.

When it comes to deferral percentages, the most asked question is "What does everyone else do?" It shouldn't surprise you to find out that answers range all across the board. In their "Annual 401(k) Benchmarking Survey (2012 Edition)," industry research firm Deloitte found "the most common default deferral percentage remained consistent from 2011 to 2012 at 3%. While a 3% deferral rate will get participants into the plan, unless it is coupled with step-up contributions and an active education campaign, 3% is not likely to support a comfortable retirement." On the other hand, Russell Investments ("A Defined Contribution Retirement Handbook – 2014/2015"), citing Plan Sponsor Council of America's "55th Annual Survey of Profit Sharing and 401k Plans, 2012," reports an average contribution rate of 6-7%.

Academic studies have long suggested why participants aggregate deferral rates around certain percentages and real-world practitioners can confirm their findings. It's called the "matching threshold" and it means people will contribute up to the percentage of the company match. Joshua Duvall, a financial planner for Capital Financial Services in Glenville, New York says, "The typical deferral rate is unfortunately only as high as the company match. For example, many employers match employee contributions into a 401k at a limit of 5%. So the employee will contribute 5% of their salary to a 401k to make sure they get the full 5% match from the employer but they won't go higher than that. From the employee's viewpoint, they don't want to leave 'free money' on the table, but they also feel like they have to live and can't be determined enough to decrease their standard of living so they can contribute more to their retirement account. It is a constant struggle for most American employees."

Courtenay Shipley, Chief Planologist at Retirement Planology, Inc. of Alexandria, Virginia, offers this explanation as to why employees defer whatever the match rate is and no higher. She says, "There's a mentality that the company match is the 'max' they should put in." She also notes, sans match, the deferral rate is much lower. If there is no match, she says the average deferral rate is "somewhere around 4% with lousy overall participation. That is usually caused by one or two people putting a lot in and a whole lot of folks not participating at all." The problem, as she sees it, is with the very nature of the "deferral rate" itself. It's not a hard dollar amount. Rather, it only reflects a percentage of someone's paycheck. "Overall, percentage rates are tricky," says Shipley. "Most people don't know or calculate out what 1% or 2% of their check is. I think there's a bit of a misconception that it's a lot of money."

Besides the "matching threshold," academics have discovered that people also set deferral rates around arbitrary numbers — normally numbers divided by 5. For example, Darryl J. Poisson, founder and president of DJP Wealth Management in Tampa, Florida, says, "I most typically see employees defer the exact same percentage as their employer matches independent of the size (2%, 6%, etc.) of the match. Outside of this phenomenon, I most commonly see deferral rates of 5% and 10%. Anecdotally, these deferral percentages lead me to believe that participants are making elections optically (10% is a nice round number) rather than consciously attempting to target their future needs."

If they're going to be arbitrary, (and they don't necessarily have to be — that's the point of using the Retirement Readiness Calculator featured in the last section of this book), is there any arbitrary deferral rate number out there that's better than the rest? The short answer is "yes," but with qualifications.

Offering a broad range, Gregory S. Ostrowski, Managing Partner of Scarborough Capital Management in Annapolis, Maryland, says, "In order to maintain a similar lifestyle from working life to retirement life, 15-20% of their annual salary is statistically what they will need to save during their working career."

There is a "textbook" answer, and it's based on a number of fairly common assumptions. Jonathan Leidy, Principal at Portico Wealth Advisors in Larkspur, California explains this when he says, "The generally accepted replacement ratio in retirement is 80% [of your salary]. Do this and your retirement savings should last about 35 years, which is at the longer end of most people's expected retirement window."

Jennifer Guillot, Marketing Director for Horizon Wealth Management in Baton Rouge, Louisiana, believes setting as a goal a 20% deferral rate "is a good idea because it slowly, over time, creates a great habit of not spending all of what you earn." She says, "It helps create a balance between enjoying the here and now and yet saving for the future. You can't forsake your future income need (a time when you may not want to or be able to earn income) merely to live it up in the here and now. Likewise, you can't forsake enjoying the here and now to save for a future income that you may never live to need. It's a delicate balance. You never know when the last grain of sand is falling through your hourglass, yet you must prepare as though you'll live a normal lifespan." She likens this to the fable of the ant and the grasshopper: "Prepare for the days of necessity. While you can still earn income, save little by little for the point in time when you'll no longer want to (or have the capacity to) earn income yet still have the need to pay bills to live your lifestyle."

Clearly, it's highly unlikely any employee will survive the sticker shock of going from saving nothing to saving 20% of their salary. Still, there are practical strategies to build up to this goal over time. Poisson says, "Participants who slowly increase deferrals over time (often on an annual basis) tend to create positive reinforcing habits. Psychologically, the impact of small, yet increasing, deferrals feels negligible. In addition, the participant benefits from positive reinforcement and a more rapidly self-funding retirement."

Sean Ciemiewicz, Principal of Retirement Benefits Group in San Diego, California, offers a well-defined process toward building up one's deferral rate. His firm doesn't pick an arbitrary target but determines the exact deferral rate needed by each investor. He says his firm "recommends deferral rates of anywhere between 12% to 15%, if the employee is able." He finds "this allows employees to have a balanced life with regards to the amount of pay they are able to take home while still saving for a comfortable retirement." In order to reach 12% and hopefully 15%, Ciemiewicz recommends that "investors slowly increase their contributions over time. I tell employees all the time, every three to six months, increase your contribution by 1%. If they follow through, there will be very little impact on their take home pay and they'll be able to adjust to the difference quite quickly. Furthermore, they'll often reach 15% within a year. People are hesitant to immediately start at 15%, but once you walk them through how to simply increase their contributions over time, it becomes a lot less burdensome."

Still not convinced you have the self-discipline to save 15%-20% a year? Well, I'm not letting you off the hook that easy. Here are:

3 Incredibly Ridiculously Easy Ways to Increase How Much You Contribute to Your Retirement Plan Every Year

1. Do You Get a Refund Every Year from Uncle Sam? Then Reduce Withholding on Your Paycheck. There are tricks employees can use to "fool" themselves into saving more. Duvall suggests one way to increase 401k contributions is "to create extra cash flow via a change in the employee's W-4. If an employee gets a large tax refund each year, they are withholding too much from their checks each pay period. Increase the allowances on your W-4, which will allocate less to taxes and you can use that extra money to contribute to your 401k. Obviously this will remove your large tax refund each year, but now you are getting a year's worth of tax-deferred growth in the 401k and you are also eliminating the interest free loan you've been giving the government every year."

2. Contribute All or Most of Your Year-End Bonus Money to Your Retirement Plan. Another trick to play involves year-end bonus money. Wayne Bland, owner of Bland Retirement Services in Charlotte, North Carolina, says, "I encourage plan sponsors that offer end of year bonuses to offer their employees the option to contribute all or a portion of their bonuses into their 401k up to the allowable limit. This increases their annual deferral without reducing take home pay."

3. Work One-on-One With an Advisor, Life Coach or other appropriate Counselor. Shipley says, "Sitting down with employees one-on-one to talk through their plan and path to get there is the best way to convince 401k savers to increase their deferral rate for several reasons. One, because they have a tangible goal to shoot for — closing the gap between what they want in the future versus what they are on track for now. Two, they are taking the time out of their schedule to focus on it so that inertia doesn't win again. Three, they are able to ask questions about their particular situation and get holistic help about their finances."

As much sense as Shipley makes, some folks just aren't in a position to save more. They shouldn't get depressed, though, as all is not lost. There's one other cold-slap-in-the-face common sense tactic that we've saved for last. Early Earl and Late Larry are fighters and aren't afraid to pull out all the stops. Remember, they have one more lever. We'll discuss the ramifications of that lever in the next chapter.

CHAPTER TWENTY-FOUR:
THE LAST ARROW IN YOUR QUIVER –
THINKING THE UNTHINKABLE (OR IS IT?)

Kevin Hall, President of BenePAY Florida, located in Clearwater, Florida, witnessed a most unique way to prod employees to increase their deferral rate. He was sitting in on a company 401k meeting when "the owner asked if anyone had ever been to a Walmart and seen the greeter at the door. Almost everyone in the room raised a hand. The owner proceeded to pull out an application for employment to Walmart and a deferral form for the 401k. He clearly stated, 'You can complete either this application for employment to be a greeter at Walmart in your later years or you can complete this deferral form to increase your contribution to your retirement plan. One or the other will likely be your financial future. It is strongly recommended you complete the deferral form unless your desire is to be a Walmart greeter in retirement.'"

The cruel reality is some people are simply not in a position to increase their contributions so that they can retire with no strings attached. Let's return to our favorite trio and see what further lessons they might provide.

In order to accumulate roughly the same amount of wealth as Turbo Tot, Early Earl and Late Larry can increase their annual contributions. But for both of them, this may prove difficult. What's the alternative? They can each pull their respective third levers and determine how much longer they would need to work to have a chance to equal what Turbo Tot has. For Early Earl, that means continuing the daily routine until he turns 85. Surprisingly, Late Larry doesn't have to put in that many more hours. He can retire when he's age 89.

How realistic is the option of working longer?

Now, before I scare you into giving up reading the rest of this book (and right when you're about to get into the section that contains the real "How-to" meat), let me take a step back. More precisely, let me take you about 120 pages back. Remember what I wrote about my own personal decision to retire. Basically, it was to continue working, but doing so on my own terms. I don't work for a boss (other than my wife and, yes, given the amount of regulation in my chosen industry, the government). I'd like to think I've grown attached to my clients so they're more like friends than clients.

It turns out I'm no different than many retirees. In fact, most pre-retirees assume they will continue working even though they are "retired." Wanna know something more surprising? They're doing so because they want to, not because they need to. Unfortunately, if you pick up a newspaper or read one of those magazines in the checkout aisle, it seems like the next generation of Americans will never be able to retire.

The foreboding doom and gloom of a less-than-perfect retirement can be found everywhere. The claim that the 401k — and thus, America's retirement system — is broken, has been repeated so often people simply assume it's a fact. In Washington, politicians are threatening to "do something" (which usually ends up making matters worse). Across the country, people talk of "working forever," "never retiring," and other such depressing sentiments.

Blame it on the lingering effects of the market collapse in 2008/2009. Blame it on the dismal economy. Blame it on the record high number of people in the labor force who aren't working. Whatever the reason, recent surveys show a vast majority of people who haven't retired yet expect to continue working into their retirement years. Despite this apparent pessimism, there is surprisingly positive news among those who have actually retired.

Nancy Collamer of Old Greenwich, Connecticut, is the founder of MyLifestyleCareer.com and author of the book *Second-Act Careers*. As you might guess, she's very familiar with what people really do when they retire. She says, "A new Merrill Lynch study shows nearly three quarters of the pre-retirees age 50 and older surveyed (72%) said their 'ideal retirement' includes work in some capacity." The Merrill Lynch study, titled "Work in Retirement: Myths and Motivations" is based on interviews with more than 7,000 respondents in March 2014.

Sounds like a lot of people are planning to work during their retirement years, right? A funny thing happens though, once you pick up that gold watch. "Almost three-fourths of Americans state they wouldn't mind working some in retirement. However, this drops down in retirement," says Jamie Hopkins.

Several surveys confirm what Hopkins is saying. Adam Jordan, Director of Investment Research and Management at Paul Ried Financial Group, LLC in Bellevue, Washington says, "According to the Employee Benefit Research Institute's (EBRI) 2014 Retirement

Confidence Survey, the percentage of retirees who work for pay, in one form or another, is 27%." In fact, EBRI's survey, like the Merrill Lynch survey, also showed a supermajority (65%) of pre-retirees expect to work in retirement.

"According to AARP, approximately 22% of retirees continue to work at least part-time in retirement," says Pamela J. Sams, Chartered Retirement Planning Counselor at Jackson Sams Financial Services in Herndon, Virginia. The AARP Study also shows that among pre-retirees, half expect to continuing working at least part-time for the rest of their lives.

People have different reasons for wanting to stay in the work force. "Some retirees continue to earn outside income out of necessity; the income from other sources is not sufficient to maintain the standard of living they hoped for," says Richard Sturm, a financial adviser, educator and public speaker in Seal Beach, California. "But," he continues, "other retirees earn outside income to remain active. Some retirees find that they are not remaining as active as they thought they might following retirement, so they seek out part-time jobs to stay busy."

Sean Moore, Vice President at Alter Retirement Planning in Boca Raton, Florida, sees the same thing. He says, "Some found themselves in that situation because a job loss or corporate downsizing forced them to retire earlier than expected. Others have a tough time adjusting to spending less money while retired. Some people like to work. They enjoy the human interaction and having a routine helps them feel 'normal.' Not everyone wants to sit on the front porch in their golden years."

"With our clients," says Jordan, "it is generally not a financially motivated decision but a lifestyle decision. They have a desire to stay mentally engaged in an activity that they enjoy and oftentimes it helps them stay socially active as well."

It's not surprising to see different motivators for different people who decide to work during their retirement years. For some, it's just poor planning and bad luck. Nathaniel C. Propes, Chief Investment Strategist of Capital Management Advisors in Atlanta, Georgia, says, "Retirees continue to earn outside income because they put themselves under unrealistic expectations regarding their lifestyle during retirement. They created this gap in their retirement expectations by increasing expenditures, primarily on their residence, throughout the 90s and early 2000s. Utilization of leverage on their homes caused many to find their mortgage significantly underwater at the same time that their 401k crashed and burned in the 2008-2009 collapse."

"If someone needs to work in retirement it is usually because they did not save enough early on in their careers or a major unforeseen event changed their retirement trajectory," says Hopkins. "These black swan events can be in the form of unexpected medical expenses, bad investments, early loss of a spouse, employer layoffs, or employer bankruptcy, and can represent an unknown financial impact when trying to save for retirement. Even the best laid retirement plan can be undone by a black swan event. In those cases, the retiree might have no other option than continuing to work."

Thomas Scanlon, Financial Advisor at Raymond James in Manchester, Connecticut, says, "Some retirees continue to work for health insurance and other benefits. Other retirees may be forced to continue to work due to a lack of planning. They may not have saved enough for retirement or they may be helping out children and grandchildren."

On the other hand, some people do it because it's the only thing they've ever done. "Others continue to work because they like to. They never really developed any serious hobbies and want to feel that they are still productive," says Scanlon.

Matt Jehn, Managing Partner at Royal Oak Financial Group in Columbus, Ohio, agrees. He says, "Some people don't know how to retire. They have developed a passion or desire to do something once retirement has come. Additionally, the folks working who do not really need to be working feel as though they will never have enough."

We should keep in mind the changing demographics of retirement as more and more baby boomers enter their golden years. "Today's retiree is healthier and wants to keep mentally active, so many start their dream business turning their passion or hobby into a part-time retirement business," says Joseph Leonard of Best Ideas for Retirement Businesses in Seattle, Washington.

"People are living longer, healthier lives which means that many people have at least 15-20 years after they retire," says Collamer. "What are they going to do to fill that time and how will they make their money last? Working allows them to supplement their income, while infusing their days with meaning, structure, and a routine. Working in retirement is very different from working full-time — most people pursue flexible, entrepreneurial, seasonal, and/or part-time options, rather than full-time employment."

It's not surprising that the most coddled generation in history — the me generation — won't submit to any off-the-shelf definition of retirement. "Retirement is different for each individual," says Sams. "The 'rocking chair on the porch passing the time away' is not everyone's vision of retirement. People often plan for the financials of retirement but not the lifestyle. Many retirees continue to work not because they need the income but because they are bored."

Sturm says, "For some, the idea of retirement sounds good in theory, but in practice can be lonely — especially for widowed or other single individuals. Part-time work provides an outlet for seniors to continue contributing. Other seniors find that part-time work helps keep their cognitive skills sharp."

Rachele Bouchand says, "About a quarter of my clients continue to earn outside income during their retirement years. This income is usually from board participation or working for a not-for-profit institution they're passionate about. I don't have many clients who 'need' to do this. The reason why many of my clients continue to work part-time is because they want to continue being involved in their local community and it gives them intellectual stimulation. The bottom line is that these positions are optional for them and make them happy. They choose these organizations and know that they can leave if they need to."

Don't understate the need to "do something," especially for successful people. One financial adviser, who didn't leave his name, told *FiduciaryNews.com*, "More typical is the client who has more than $2 million invested with me but after a busy and successful work life, found retirement too boring to do the more mundane retirement activities. Since he enjoyed golf, he purchased the management contract at a nearby public golf course. He is again challenged to turn around the management and earn a profit running the course."

Even if they're mathematically comfortable, there remains an emotional need that only earning income can fulfill. Diana Gardner Robinson, PhD. from Rochester, New York, offered to share her personal journey with our readers. Why does she choose to work in retirement? She says, "Based on the actuarial charts on which the IRS requires conversion from IRA, I have enough, but I don't believe that the actuarial charts are based on having a large number of female relatives, including my mother, who lived into their late nineties."

Unfortunately, her personal circumstances haven't left her with much from Social Security. "I spent 25 years married to a man who insisted that I not work so that he should be free to accept transfers/promotions and move any time he wanted to. The portion of Social Security Income that I get based on his income doesn't do it." In the end, though, despite not really "needing" outside income, it is the unknown that she fears the most. "I guess you could say it is insecurity about inflation. I don't really know if I need it or not but the point between 'need' and 'not need' is very grey." So when she decided on a source of outside income, she looked for examples among her peers. "Many of my retirement age friends are adjunct instructors/professors at universities and community colleges and/or have micro-businesses such as life coaching or do freelance writing. I do a bit of all three."

Robinson's experience with multiple outside income sources is not atypical. "Most typical outside source is part-time work," says Moore. "We have a few examples of clients turning a hobby into a source of income. Selling artwork, pet sitting, and restoring classic cars are all examples we've seen."

There is a cornucopia of choices for retirees seeking a new arena. "The sources of outside income run the gamut from golf course maintenance, to driving cars and working temp jobs. Some set up their own consulting business," says Scanlon.

"The main types of retirement work that I see come from part-time employment and self-employed individuals," says Hopkins. "More specifically, consulting work, teaching, coaching, writing, blogging, and running a small business are the main types of post-retirement employment opportunities. Additionally, many large employers such as Wal-Mart, Home Depot, and Wegmans offer part-time employment opportunities to elderly workers."

Among retirees, Collamer list includes revenues based on "Expert-based income such as consulting, coaching, teaching, writing, and speaking. One area where I see a lot of opportunity is entrepreneurial support services. While entrepreneurs are skilled at their core business (e.g., a plumber knows how to fix your pipes) most entrepreneurs need help with running, marketing, and managing their business. They also need help with a variety of tasks on a part-time basis — bookkeeping, writing press releases, designing logos, writing their blog posts, etc."

"A lot of retirees are starting their own businesses," says Sams. "Consulting, starting bed & breakfast establishments, and turning their hobbies into a business. Others will work at places with flexible hours such as tour guides at museums, Walmart greeters, and libraries."

Don't overlook the different opportunities available in different regions of the country. "In our area, seniors choose local amusement parks because of the flexibility in scheduling," says Sturm. "I have known other retirees who have purchased an RV and travel the country working for RV parks. These arrangements often provide them with extra income and free space rentals."

One of the most fruitful enterprises is to take advantage of a career's worth of experience. Joanne Cleaver, President of Wilson-Taylor Associates, Inc. in Chicago, Illinois and author of *The Career Lattice*, runs a series of workshops "designed for career shifting late in life and as a retirement transition plan." Participants in these workshops, she says, "want to work a bit longer, but at a different job, to either avoid tapping their savings, or to continue adding to it. My advice is to abandon the popular myth of career reinvention, which assumes that you'll start over from scratch with a new career in a new field. That's dumb because you have a lifetime of experience and connections to build on. If you are looking to gain significant income from ages 55–70, you have to make the most of what you have. You don't have enough time to start over."

Collamer reminds us what retirement means to many people. She says, "In doing the research for *Second-Act Careers*, I spoke at length with nearly 40 people, most of whom were in their 50s and 60s, who were having the time of their lives working in their second acts. And even though they typically no longer earn what they once did, they are energized, engaged, and connected to their communities; they feel valued, are learning new skills, and know they are making a difference. When asked how long they planned to continue working, the vast majority said they have no intention of slowing down anytime soon; they are simply having too much fun."

Modern Retirement isn't a make-believe TV series on ABC. It's being played out in cities and towns from coast-to-coast in America. For many, it involves working either in volunteer positions or in positions that earn money. For some, it means a second or perhaps a third career. Even if your financial position suggests you can lie on the beach all day, don't count on doing that. Working during retirement is not something to be feared. As Collamer says, it should be a way to continue "having too much fun."

I know you're chomping at the bit asking, So, what's between today and me 'having too much fun'?" Or, another way of saying that is "Hey! What's my number?" The next section reveals how you can easily discover the answer by yourself (or, if you prefer, with the help of a financial expert). But there's something you've got to really know before you can start (if you don't, then I would highly recommend you work with a professional who does).

SECTION FIVE:

– MY PERSONAL PLAN –

A PENCIL, SOME PERSONAL DATA, AND A CALCULATOR ARE ALL YOU NEED TO DISCOVER YOU OWN PERSONAL MAGICAL NUMBER!

Chapter Twenty-Five:
Why Everyday People Hate and Mistrust
the Financial Services Industry

Volatility never cut it in terms of defining investor risk. As we learned in Chapter Sixteen (and *Appendix III* if you were ambitious), the founders of MPT ("Modern Portfolio Theory" if you've forgotten, which to be honest, as with all other investment-related jargon, it's not a bad idea to forget) recognized the flaws of describing risk in terms of volatility. Volatility covered both ends of the risk/return trade-off. When volatility caused investors to miss their target, this was the realization of downside risk. When volatility caused investors to meet or exceed their target, this was the realization of upside potential (i.e., return).

That single term — volatility — stood to account for both the downside risk as well as the upside potential for any particular investment. That those responsible for creating MPT used this specific statistic to denote risk stands as their greatest failure. So close, yet so far.

I say "close" because the key for correctly identifying risk lies within the very components of volatility. We all know no one considers meeting or exceeding your goal as an example of risk. If anything, they'd call that the reward. On the other hand, most will agree, at the very least, risk can best be described as the chances you might miss your goal.

To the extent "risk" reflects the relative danger associated with missing a specific goal, then merely reducing it to the odds of missing your target understates its true significance.

Here's what I mean.

Suppose you say your goal is to walk from Point A to Point B. In this case, if you trip and fall anywhere between point A and Point B then you will have failed to meet your goal. Let's say you have a 10% chance of tripping. If you're going to define risk just as the odds of failing, then you might say you have a 10% risk.

Does this sound simple? Does it sound easy to calculate?

It is. And that's one of the attractions of using standard deviation, variance, and all those fun statistical numbers. They possess that mathematical elegance and tantalizingly close to common-sense allure the industry loves and their clients don't hesitate to believe.

Except, again, there's one nagging problem. It fails to accurately reflect the true sense of danger an investor might be in. It explains why the big boys in the financial industry don't understand, after the epic market collapse of 2008/2009, that people hate them. They still think they told investors about the risks. According to the way they define risk, they did. Their risk-tolerance questionnaires said so. Trouble is, the rest of the world doesn't define risk that way.

To show this, I'll return to our walking analogy.

I'll keep the basic concept the same. The goal is to walk from Point A to Point B. Only this time, I'll present three different scenarios. In each scenario, though, the subject will walk on a similarly flat surface, so the probability of falling remains 10%.

- In Scenario I, Subject I is walking on a sturdy floor.
- In Scenario II, Subject II is walking atop a string of sturdy three-foot high boxes.
- In Scenario III, Subject III is walking on the sturdy ledge of a skyscraper thirty stories above the hustle and bustle below.

Which subject engages in the riskiest endeavor?

Remember, they all have an equal chance of falling. If you were to use statistics similar to MPT, (like many in the industry still do), then you would say they all share the same risk. Unfortunately, if you're like most people, saying they all share the same risk would be like hearing fingernails scratching along a blackboard. Despite the mathematical clarity of the shared 10% probability of failing, it just doesn't feel right to say they each have the same risk.

Here's why. What happens if each subject fails to meet his goal? If Subject I falls, the worst that could happen in most likelihood is that he'd twist his ankle. If Subject II falls, he just might break his leg. Finally, if Subject III falls, well let's just say you don't have to be a Wallenda to know what happens then.

Focusing on the consequences of failing to meet the goal rather than merely the odds of failing to meet the goal paints a very different picture when it comes to assessing risk. The probable outcome of failing to meet the goal looks like this: Subject I twists his ankle; Subject II breaks his leg; and, Subject III dies.

I'll ask it again. Which subject engages in the riskiest endeavor? All of those who answered "Subject III" will immediately know why I have a fear of flying. Thus is revealed the new paradigm that begins to show how we should really define "risk." I put the term "risk" in quotes because I don't think that's the best word to use anymore. I think it will forever be associated with odds and probability — as well it should be. What it doesn't connote is the clear assessment of danger this new paradigm must measure. You cannot begin to create a meaningful personal plan until you learn how to measure what happens when you fail to meet a goal. We'll talk about a better name for this type of failure and just what exactly this has to do with my fear of flying in the next chapter.

CHAPTER TWENTY-SIX:
"PERIL" — THE NEW "RISK"

I've been told by nearly everyone I meet that my fear of flying is irrational. They point to endless statistics showing how flying is much safer than driving cars. I agree with their statistics, but, then again, they're just statistics. They don't measure the true "risk" of flying.

There's that word again. "Risk." Risk is perhaps the most overused and abused word in the investment business. It has rightfully earned a bad rap due to its unfortunate association with MPT techniques. It has been misused in the form of "risk tolerance" questionnaires of dubious relevance. "Risk," together with "volatility," has just about been labeled a universally accepted mathematical failure.

The trouble with the word "risk" is that it doesn't accurately describe the true danger of a situation. "Risk" is a word forever associated with chance, odds, and probability in general. (In case you doubt this, look up its definition.) It's not the odds of failure that's important. It's what happens in the event of failure. "Risk" simply doesn't measure the consequences of failure. What we need is a new word — a word that encompasses both the sense of "exposure" to the downside as well as a sense of "magnitude" should that downside become reality.

I, for one, nominate the word "peril." I would have nominated "jeopardy" but I'm pretty sure Alex Trebek owns all North American first use rights to the word. So, "peril" it is. According to Random House, "peril" not only means "exposure to injury" (as in the probability of failure), but is also means "something that causes or may cause injury" (as in the consequences of failure). It appears well suited to replace "risk" as our preferred term to describe the impact of failing to meet a goal.

Let's return to my fear of flying. I assure you, my reasoning behind this fear is sound. Yes, it's more likely I'll be involved in an automobile accident than in an airplane accident. But what is the likelihood of survival in either accident. I walked away from one major car accident (it totaled my brand new truck) and any number of minor accidents. I doubt I could say the same should I ever be involved in an aeronautical mishap.

In this sense, flying presents a much greater peril than does driving a car. In fact, citing their own exclusive study, *USA Today* reported ("Air Crash Survival Rates Haven't Improved Since the '70s," August 9, 2013), "During all phases of flight, the study found, just 4% of people aboard U.S. airline flights survived fatal accidents from Jan. 1, 2000, through July 10, 2013." Statistics from the National Highway Traffic Safety Administration showed there were 5.4 million non-fatal car crashes each year and only 35,000 fatal accidents, yielding a survival rate of more than 99%. Think about it: 4% vs. 99+%. Now do you understand the difference between peril and risk?

Let's apply this same sense to investments. If you have a goal to reach $1,000 and you currently have $910, you'll need to earn 10% on your original money to get to $1,000. Let's say you only earn 9%. You'd be ten dollars short. If you're like many people, you could probably scrounge up $10 without much trouble. Missing your goal isn't that much of a problem.

What if we did the same thing except your goal is to reach $1,000,000 and you're starting with $910,000. You earn only 9% making you about $10,000 short. That's a pretty big shortfall. Not many people go around carrying that much loose change in their wallets. In this latter case, the $1,000,000 investor would be in much greater peril than the $1,000 investor, even though they both missed their 10% return target by the same amount.

Retirement investors are more like the $1,000,000 investor. While they are fortunate to have decades to reach their lofty goal, failure to miss their return target by even a smidgen can have grave consequences.

We don't need a system that measures your risk. We need a system that measures your peril.

Incidentally, there's one other problem with MPT that this new paradigm removes. It no longer relies on investment statistics as part of the individual investor equation. The new paradigm only requires the investor to define his goal and what's needed to achieve that goal. That alone allows the investor to determine the true peril of failing to meet that goal. The variability of investments then becomes a tool, not part of the assessment.

What is this new system some of the leading investment advisers use today to work within the parameters of this new paradigm? In the next chapter I'll reveal its name and tell you how these pioneers are using it right now to help retirement savers make the best plans.

CHAPTER TWENTY-SEVEN:
THE NEW WAY: GOAL-ORIENTED TARGETING

Rather than focusing on risk, some professionals feel it's better to focus on the saver's Goal-Oriented Target ("GOT"), i.e., the specific return requirements needed to attain specific goals. "If savers can't identify their goal, then the 401k statement that comes in the mail is just a series of numbers and meaningless data. What you can do with those numbers, or plan to do, can help a saver achieve long-term success," says Kevin Conard.

As achieving goals represent the whole purpose of making a plan, for some, using the GOT method is critical. "It's better to speak of risk in terms of failing to meet the goal-oriented target because that's what counts!" says Andrew Carrillo, CEO & President of Barnett Capital Advisors in Miami, Florida.

Jeremy C. Brenn, Vice President at Sensenig Capital Advisors, Inc. in Philadelphia, Pennsylvania, also thinks it's better to speak of "risk" in terms of failing to meet a specific GOT. He says, "It helps to discuss risk in this fashion because it educates regular savers on the things they should be focusing on versus what they have no control over. Our view is that we can't control markets, the returns they provide, or the subsequent volatility. But, we can control our ability to save and invest regularly, our ability to stay disciplined during tough market environments, etc." Sound familiar?

For Boersen, he first shows clients "the 'risk' of not reaching the investment return goal (i.e., GOT) and what that means for retirement projections." He says, "This simple step is useful for savers who want to shy away from equity and more towards low-yielding fixed income for safety despite having two or more decades before retirement. After a market drop, we still show the modeling but for a different reason. We show it to illustrate the minimal impact a 10% or 20% drop has on 20–30 year plans. A temporary drop typically only impacts the 'investment return needed to reach goals' by less than half a percentage point due to time horizons."

Stokes agrees. She says, "We define risk as the chance that you will not meet your goals. Risk is living longer than your money. Volatility fails as a definition for 'risk' because the real 'risk' is outliving your resources. For example, a Certificate of Deposit has low volatility, but carries incredible purchasing power risk — meaning you are almost guaranteed to lose to inflation and rising costs over the long term. In terms of outliving your resources, CD's are incredibility risky — much more so than a well-built stock portfolio."

Aside from its purely mathematical significance, incorporating the GOT discipline also helps with saving psychology. Alfidi says, "Using a GOT keeps savers focused on the long term. They need to stop worrying about the 'risk' of short-term swings in asset values."

Hopkins agrees. He likes the idea of focusing on a single GOT — and whether or not you can achieve that — as the benchmark for investors. He goes a step further, though, when he indicts the intricate mathematical models commonly used by purveyors of MPT. He says, "When planning and investing for long periods of time, volatility as a measure of risk becomes less important. If you can ride out down markets, you can ignore some of the volatility risk inherent with certain investments. Instead, focusing on the likelihood of failing to meet a specified goal-oriented target can be a better way to frame risk. For example, simulations based on game theory (called "Monte Carlo simulations") will give you the likelihood of meeting a projected outcome. While this can be extremely helpful in crafting a plan, it is usually not the best way to present the plan or strategy to the investor because it focuses on the percent change of success or failure of a particular strategy. Ultimately, this type of analysis misses out on how much you miss the target, either over or under."

Speaking of mathematics, it is from that standpoint that the GOT is similar in concept to the way trustees manage corporate pensions. There, the GOT is called the "actuarial assumption." The actuarial assumption is derived from a series of variables. Into this complicated cauldron goes data such as age, gender, life expectancy, expected rates of return, and prevailing interest rates. And out comes this magic number. The fact that it's called an "actuarial assumption" should give you a hint as to the degree of confidence people have in it. That's because the source of all this data is an ever-changing hard-to-pin-down population. At best, it's a really good guess on how things should turn out. Given this uncertainty, trustees will often ask professional money managers to manage the portfolio to this particular number.

Similarly, one's GOT can also be calculated using a set of variables. "The GOT must be liability-driven over a specified timeline," says Alfidi. He compares calculating a GOT with pensions when he says, "Longitudinal demographic studies matter as the ultimate underpinning of liability-driven investing for pension plans." That's a mouthful! Allow me to explain.

Creating a Goal-Oriented Target needn't be rocket science (and, as a trained astrophysicist, I ought to know). This is especially true for retirement-oriented goals. As we mentioned at the outset, there is plenty of demographic history to give everyone a good sense for their own personal retirement Goal-Oriented Target. It's only a matter of identifying the right numbers. Conard says, "We simply start by picking an age at which they would like to retire. As long as the date doesn't move significantly, their portfolio allocation shouldn't either."

Beyond retirement, though, calculating a GOT can get tricky. "In order to figure out what an investor's target should be," says Hopkins, "you need to understand where this investment fits into the overall financial plan and strategy of the investor. Is this investment being used to generate future income or is it being used to generate wealth? These are important questions that help determine how the investment strategy should be derived for a specific goal."

Still, using the GOT process for non-retirement goals does help and, given simple goals, can be straightforward and easy to understand. Carbone says, "The emphasis is placed on what the client is trying to achieve rather than what is going on, for instance, with the S&P 500. To take an example, if a client has a short term housing goal, it is not relevant how the S&P 500 is performing compared to the client's short term investment goals."

Overall, Boersen sees GOT as a useful method for reframing the idea of what's important, especially for retirement savers. He says, "Getting people to think about goals as opposed to short term returns is helpful as it changes their viewpoint. The savers with short viewpoints are the ones who typically act contrary to their long-term financial success. By refocusing on long-term goals we take the focus off of day-to-day, or even month-to-month, movements. Our retirement planning focus typically helps clients refocus on the long-term."

Even a well-documented GOT is no guarantee of success. Still, Stokes prefers it to another popular form of portfolio construction. She says, "You may have a 'target return' that is necessary to meet your goals, but there is nothing that will guarantee that you will meet those goals. There is no such thing as a future fact — the future is unknowable. However, backing into a proper allocation based on how much volatility and return you may need makes much more sense than focusing on what you can tolerate. Using 'risk tolerance' alone to decide a proper portfolio is not just wrong, it's damaging."

Charles Murphy, VP & CFO at American Investment Services, Inc. in Great Barrington, Massachusetts, says, "It is better to speak of risk in terms of failing to meet a goal rather than just volatility as an advisor can speak about how you might not reach that goal given the current specific investments or investment plan or lack of. Goals give an investor a clearer plan and picture of how to get where they want to go rather than just speaking about reducing volatility for return."

The GOT process gives clients something they can really get their hands onto. Grishman says, "Simply put, it makes it real. When the industry uses fabricated or misleading jargon like 'volatility,' most people just check out and do nothing. When we tie risk to real-life objectives, or failure to meet those objectives, it becomes a priority to handle the risk and minimize it."

Carrillo takes a methodological approach when determining a client's GOT. "I ask investors about their dreams and goals," he says. "I then calculate the income they would need in today's dollars, and then factor in inflation to arrive at the rate of return and savings needs necessary to reach their goals."

In the end, calculating one's GOT may be as simple as using a specialized retirement calculator (I'll introduce such a specialized retirement calculator in Chapter Thirty: the "Retirement Readiness Calculator"). "The absolute best way to derive their goal-oriented target," says Freeman, "is by way of a financial plan, or at the very least, a retirement calculator. This 'hurdle rate' then helps them understand what return must be accomplished to achieve their goals. It also helps them understand that if too much risk is taken and things go awry, their goals may need to negatively change."

By now we've gotten to know each other pretty well. I'm guessing you're wondering "Just how does this 'Goal-Oriented Targeting' paradigm work?" and "What can it tell me about the appropriateness of my plan?" and "How exactly does the darn thing worl?" It's pretty easy to understand, especially if you've spent many hours watching late (and I mean late) night TV. Here's what I mean...

CHAPTER TWENTY-EIGHT:
HOW DOES GOAL-ORIENTED
TARGETING WORK?

Ever notice those clever late night TV ads. They always shout out how you "only" have to pay five "easy" installments of $25 (actually "$24.95"). They never tell you the darn thing costs $125.00. Why do you think this is so?

You know full well why. You know most people see "$25" and think "$25." (OK, so they really see "24.95" and think "$24.") You know they don't do the math and think $125. You also know "$25" (or "$24") gets their attention while $125 makes them turn the channel. Essentially, big numbers tend to scare people away. Numbers with six digits or more? Well, most people just don't swim in that pool. In fact, even five digits may be foreign to a lot of people. On the other hand, they're more comfortable with the small numbers they see every day. It's a fairly standard marketing tactic, long accepted by salesman and consumers alike.

This tells you why the "What's Your Number" commercial that showed those really big numbers (usually seven or eight figures — that's $1 million+) didn't inspire folks. This fact alone demonstrates to us what's wrong with Wall Street's advertising agencies. It also explains why Goal-Oriented Targeting works.

Here. I'll show you. Let's say you're 28 years old and you've been working for a really nice company for five years. You're making a cool $62,500 a year. Under most rules of thumb, the projected retirement income you need is 80% of your salary. In your case, that's $50,000. Let's say you think you can earn 3% a year once you retire. That's a reasonable return, right? After all, the average return of stocks in the long run is a whopping 10%, so 3% sounds not only doable, but almost too small. Let's also say you want your projected income need to equal 5% of your total retirement assets when you retire (that's what many experts advise). Given this and a 3% annual return rate, you won't run out of money for 31 years after you retire. Do you expect to live past 101? If so, let's increase that annual return rate to 4% (remember, we thought 3% might have been too small to begin with). In this case, you get to live to 110 before you run out of money. Sound good enough to you?

OK, well, here's the kicker. In order for this to work you need to save a total of $1,000,000.

Under the "What's Your Number?" scenario in that infamous commercial, that's the number that floats above your head: $1,000,000. Look at it. Look at it again. Here, maybe this will help:

$$\$1,000,000.^{00}$$

Unless you're a Rockefeller (hmm, that expression might be too old for some to understand), those seven digits represent something you only see when playing Monopoly. That's one big honkin' number. It's the stuff lotteries are made of. It's not for us regular folks. Heck, you barely have $19,000 in your 401k and you're only putting away well less than $2,000 a year ($1,875, to be exact). Given this reality, the typical response when people see a number this large is, "Not me. Ain't gonna happen."

But wait! Remember those late night TV commercials that offered such great deals. Well, have I got a deal for you. It's called Goal-Oriented Targeting and here's how it works.

Since your company matches one-for-one up to 3% of your salary, you decided long ago to contribute that same 3% of your salary. That's your $1,875 annual contribution. Of course, you need to add your company's match, so the total amount of money contributed to your account every year is $3,750. Adding up all those annual contributions over the next 42 years (did I tell you you're retiring at the age of 70) gives you only $157,500, well below the required million dollars. You can add in your current total ($19,000) and that gives you $176,500, still roughly six times less than what you need.

Now, if you believe Social Security will still be around by the time you retire, then, based on Social Security's Quick Estimator Calculator, the Government will chip in more than half of your projected retirement need ($31,092). That's a good thing. But, even with Social Security, you've still got to more than double your money.

By now, you're probably asking "What's the catch? There's gotta be a catch." Well, there is. Given all these numbers (and, granted, I've been throwing around a lot of them — that's why it's good to have a professional riding shotgun with you when you do this) what's the average annual return needed to meet your goal.

Wait for it...

It's 2.97% per year.

Remember what we said about 3% per year being a ridiculously low expectation for an annual return. Well, that's all you need.

Think about it. If, instead of leading with that big ol' seven-digit number like that commercial did, when you ask me, "Hey! What's My Number?" what if I answered "3%," as in, "you only need to keep doing what you're doing and earn a minimum investment return of 3% on average every year."

You can do 3%, right? Heck, you can probably do a lot more. If you can make it to an average 6.17% a year (still a reasonably low number since the average return on stocks is 10% a year), then you don't even have to worry about Social Security — you won't need it!

Goal-Oriented Targeting works because it changes the point of view from which we talk about our retirement account. No longer do we focus on big numbers or total assets. Sure, those numbers are still out there if you want to see them, but since they act as de-motivators for most people, we'll stay focused on our Goal-Oriented Target numbers.

And you should, too.

I can't tell you how many times I've seen people walk into a retirement planning meeting dour and depressed only to leave all smiles and with a bounce in their step. That's the power of Goal-Oriented Targeting. It re-orients your thinking to make achieving your own comfortable retirement much more obtainable.

Sure, Goal-Oriented Targeting works because it's easy to understand a smaller number than a larger number. But how do you know what that goal should be based on? How will you know if you're ready to retire or what you have to do to be ready to retire when you want to? Those are pretty important questions. Believe it or not, researchers and professionals believe they know the answer. I'll share what they say in the next chapter.

CHAPTER TWENTY-NINE:
ARE YOU READY TO RETIRE?

One day, while walking down the street, you meet a man who you'd swear looks exactly like Bill Gates. You know Bill Gates? You saying that name is like your grandparents saying the name "Rockefeller" (remember, he's the guy who's used to seeing numbers with a lot of zeroes behind them). Sure, you know Bill Gates. Microsoft founder. Richest man in the world. Likes to give money away. That's the one.

Funny thing, though. It turns out this fellow not only looks like Bill Gates, but he is Bill Gates. After you realize you've been staring at him a little bit longer than politeness would dictate, you meekly wave "hello" to him. He waves back and then — Surprise! — he begins to speak to you.

"Excuse me," he says, "but would you like some money?"

You stop dead in your tracks. Is he serious? Is there a trick? It is Bill Gates after all and you know he likes to share his wealth. Still awestruck by the fact you're in a conversation with a celebrity, all you can spurt out is a tentative, "Sure."

Bill smiles at you. "Great!" he says. "You're an average person, right?"

"Well, yeah," you answer.

A bit more excited, Bill giggles to himself and says, "I'm going to give you a choice between two amounts of money. If you pick the larger sum, you get to keep it?"

"And if I guess wrong?" you ask suspiciously.

"Nothing," assures Bill. "You just walk on your merry way as if this conversation never happened. So, are you ready?"

"OK," you say.

Bill shakes his head a little bit too enthusiastically, as if he's channeling his inner Joe Pesci. "OK, OK, so here's your choice. When you retire at age 68, I can either give you $100,000 in a lump sum right there on the spot, or," he pauses, "I can give you $500 a month for the rest of your life. Which one is larger?"

If you're like most people, you'd choose the hundred grand right on the spot. If you're like most people, then, you'd be wrong. A lump sum of $100,000 is not larger than $500 a month for the rest of your life.

Now, I know there are a few of you out there who picked the monthly payment. I can see you smiling smugly as your hands clutch this book more firmly. Well, I've got bad news. You're wrong, too.

You see, according to standard actuarial tables (using a 3% interest rate assumption), a lump sum of $100,000 at age 65 exactly equals receiving $500 per month for the rest of your life. At least that's what researchers say who studied this, (Goldstein, Daniel G. and Hershfield, Hal E. and Benartzi, Shlomo, "The Illusion of Wealth and Its Reversal," January 28, 2014). Simply stated, they showed that if you describe the same monetary value in two different ways, you'll get two different (and opposite) reactions from the typical person. For example, these researchers have determined, for the average person retiring at age 65, there is no mathematical difference between receiving a single lump sum payment of $100,000 versus receiving a payment of $500 per month for life. Despite their financial equivalence, the average person would see the $100,000 lump sum as the more adequate of the two.

The paper focuses on reframing this "Illusion of Wealth" from the point of view that people need to see numbers presented in a way they can better understand. Without a sophisticated financial calculator, it's hard for the professional, let alone the average person, to know when a lump sum is adequate to fund retirement. By looking at a monthly payout figure, people can more easily determine if they can cover their monthly expenses. This is why, when presented with a choice between two numbers (e.g., receiving a lump sum of $1.6 million or $10,217 a month for the rest of your life – again, mathematically equivalent amounts), people tended to pick the monthly payment instead of the lump sum. Why did they switch from the lump sum to the monthly payout? The researchers believe it's because people see the larger monthly payments as more likely to cover their monthly expense.

The trouble is, many expenses (like property taxes, insurance premiums, etc.) are annual expenses, not monthly expenses. That means you don't pay the same amount of expenses every month. Unless you're very, very, good at keeping track of your cash flow, it's a whole lot easier to think in terms of the annual income needed to cover annual expenses. There's an industry "rule" regarding this that I'll focus on for the rest of this chapter. It's a little controversial, as I'll explain in a moment, but it's what really drives everything we do from here on. To make things more exciting, here's a teaser...

[For best effect, read with one of those deep bellowing Voice-of-God baritones you hear in movie trailers.]

> *"It's been around so long, many have begun to question whether it has any basis in reality or is simply another urban legend. The fact it's often cited as "the textbook" number only detracts from its credibility. Yet, nearly every retirement adviser, financial planner, and tax consultant faithfully follows this rule. Some may question it, only to return to it as a convenient proxy. What is it? Where is it used? How has it been justified? And why could it be the single most critical data element standing between your comfortable retirement and working longer?"*

I'm talking about the "80% Salary Replacement Rule." It's one of the important assumptions financial professionals make when determining how successful a retirement savings program will be. It's used to calculate how much money retirement savers must contribute to their retirement plans. It's also a key component when computing your Goal-Oriented Target.

Although it's often referred to as "the textbook number," the true source of the number habitually goes unmentioned. The process for determining this "replacement ratio" has been in existence for more than three decades. It began early in the Reagan administration. "We built on methodology established in the 1981 President's Commission on Pension Policy, but then updated it with key findings from the Aon/Georgia State Replacement Ratio studies," says Rob Austin, Director of Retirement Research at Aon Hewitt in Charlotte, North Carolina.

Austin says, "The research starts by assuming a participant will want to maintain the same standard of living after retirement. Specifically, this means that current income is adjusted for expected changes at retirement including: elimination of retirement savings; changes in taxes; and, changes in expenditures including medical costs. Overall, this methodology produces an average need in the first year of retirement of 85% of pay."

In fact, the replacement ratio does vary from year to year as well as across the range of salaries. The number is higher for higher salaries because, at those salary levels, Social Security replaces a smaller percentage of the salary. Of course, higher income folks may also have greater discretionary spending; hence, a better shot at reducing spending in retirement — if they want to (a big if). Still, the 80% rule of thumb is actually fairly sound. It also has the benefit of being an easier number to work with (it being divisible by ten). For many professionals, however, it really suggests more of a guideline. While it represents a good (and, as we've seen, an empirically justified) starting point, specific circumstances based on the individual lifestyle choices of retirement savers may require adjustments to the number.

David Rae says, "Exceptions to the 80% rule are people who are entering retirement with a paid-off house, with a low tax base, and low cost of living." On the other hand, Rae says, "Those who want to retire early should save even more. If your health is good and you retire early, I'm going to assume you are going to have a very active retirement. The more active you are, the more likely you are to be spending on things like travel. On the opposite side, if your health is poor, you may spend even more on health care costs. The biggest threat is poor health that won't kill you. That means high medical bills for a long time."

What happens if a retirement saver hasn't saved enough, based on whatever replacement ratio they use? Daniel Cassidy, Managing Director at P-Solve in Boston, Massachusetts, says retirement savers will adjust by "working longer, lowering their standard of living, moving to a lower expense state, moving in with children, and all the normal things people will do to adjust when a budget is not met."

One of the objectives retirement savers should have is to review their specific situation at least once a year or whenever a life-changing event occurs. (This, by the way, is another one of those "rules of thumb" the textbook demands you follow.) An annual review allows the saver to identify any exceptions to the 80% Salary Replacement Rule sooner rather than later. How can one expect to see these exceptions? Rich Rausser says, "In some cases, this is the result of a well thought-out plan. In other cases, it is hard to see some of this coming, but it highlights the need to be as prepared as you can by saving earlier and more often."

Rob Drury Executive Director of the Association of Christian Financial Advisors in San Antonio, Texas, sums up what many in the industry believe when he says, "The 80 percent rule is probably a pretty reasonable benchmark, and one I've seen to be fairly reliable; but I question why, with all the modeling tools available, one should not plan using more specific figures. Granted, any method relies on speculative assumptions, but the better the numbers and the methodology going into the planning, the more reliable that planning will likely be."

Are you ready to retire? Have you saved up enough to pay yourself 80% of your salary for the rest of your life (which could be up to thirty years after you retire)? If you haven't, do you know what it takes to get there? Hey! Do you know *your* number? Are you ready to punt these hypothetical cases and start working on your own Goal-Oriented Target? If so, grab some paper, a pencil and your most recent statement (we'll provide the calculator) and turn the page. It's time to peek into your future.

CHAPTER THIRTY:
YOUR KEY PERSONAL DATA

Say "hello" to your little friend to the left here. From here on, you and he will be taking various journeys and explorations. You won't discover hidden civilizations or alien life forms, but you may just uncover the path to a comfortable retirement. This is what I call the *Hey! What's My Number?* Retirement Readiness Calculator. The real thing is a little bit more colorful. It's available on various websites (identified in Chapter Thirty Three) and the logo may be different. If you're curious, this is the original — the one that started it all!

I developed this for my large group presentations. The Retirement Readiness Calculator allows everyone in the audience to pull out their smart phone, tablet, or laptop computer and play along with me. In this way, I rely less on the PowerPoint (if you don't know why that's important, re-read the Introduction of this book) and more on the audience having fun putting in their own numbers.

And just what are those numbers? Well, they're all pretty much at your fingertips. They could be on your weekly paycheck, in your annual W-2 Form, or in your periodic 401k participant statement. To get started, you want to collect the most recent figures of the following data:

1. **Current Annual Salary** — This is quite simply the gross (i.e., before the government takes out any taxes) amount you get paid every year. You can get this from your annual W-2 form.

From this we'll determine your projected annual retirement income need by multiplying your Current Annual Salary by 80% (see previous chapter).

2. **Current Value of All Retirement Savings** — This is literally all your retirement savings. Include your current employer's 401k, any 401k's you've left at companies you used to work for as well as any IRAs of any type. You can also include taxable savings and investment accounts (like what you might have at a bank, broker, or mutual fund) if you intend to use that money for retirement. As such, this information comes from a variety of sources, including your periodic 401k statement, any relevant brokerage or mutual fund statements and any relevant bank statements. One thing not to include here is money from "rainy day" (i.e., emergency) accounts, college savings accounts, or any other pre-designated short-term savings needs.

3. **Current Annual Contribution** — This is going to be equal to both your annual contribution and your company's annual matching contribution. Most people forget to put in the company match. In fact, most people have forgotten what the company match is. If this isn't easily identifiable from your periodic 401k statement, now is a good time to give your HR department a call to ascertain how much money your company is contributing on your behalf.

4. **How Many Years Until Retirement** — Under the current rules with Social Security, you can begin taking out money at age 62, but you'll get a bump-up if you wait until you're either 66 or 67 years-old (depending on when you were born). This is what Social Security considers the "normal" retirement age. There's another bump-up at age 70, so there's an extra bonus for waiting.

You'll want to enter these numbers into the appropriate spaces on the calculator. I've chopped up my graphic of the calculator to show you specifically where you can enter the data. As you can see, I've even set aside a column for your spouse's data if you're married. Note you only have one space to enter in years until retirement. Now, I know what

Hey! What's My Number?
Retirement Readiness Calculator

Enter Your Current Data (Spouse is Optional):

	Self	Spouse
Gross Annual Salary		
Retirement Savings		
Annual Contribution		
Year to Retirement		

you're thinking, "What if my spouse doesn't retire the same year I do?" Well, since we're concerned with you (and only you) enter in the number of years *you* have until *you* retire. You can do a second calculation for your spouse based on the date your spouse expects to retire. Or, to keep things simple, just combine your assets together and enter them in the left column.

You might notice the section underneath. This contains your Projected Retirement Income Need. Your Projected Retirement Income Need is equal to your annual expenses that occur once you retire. Don't enter anything in here yet. The calculator will

Projected Retirement Income Need (Calculated)		Override? Yes No

automatically determine this figure and display it once you hit the "Press to Calculate" button. The automatic calculation uses the 80% Rule we discussed in the previous chapter. The rule takes your Gross Annual Salary (which you entered in the first line) and multiplies it by 80%. That's the number that appears here. I've included the Projected Retirement Income Need for two reasons: one, to show you its value so you can determine if it makes sense given your own familiarity with your annual expenses; and, two, so you can override it if you feel your retirement expenses will be significantly more or less that what's derived from the 80% Rule.

The next section of the calculator contains places to record your outside annual income sources. These would include income that you would receive from sources other than your own retirement savings. We don't include inheritances, lottery winnings or any other one-time lump sum payments because they can go immediately into that pile of money you have designated to pay for your retirement. (In other words, you can save money for retirement both in tax deferred vehicles like IRAs and 401k plans, and you can also save money for retirement in regular taxable accounts like bank accounts, brokerage accounts, or mutual fund accounts.)

The most likely source of outside income comes from Social Security. The Social Security Administration used to mail your current expected payments based on various retirement ages every year on your birthday. Now you can go on-line and get that information. Enter the annualized figures from both spouses if you're married. (Remember, Social Security reports what it pays you on a monthly basis. You'll need to take that number and multiply it by 12 to get the number you're supposed to

Enter Your Post-Retirement Projections (Optional):		
Social Security		
Pensions		
Outside Income		

enter here.) The next most likely source of outside income is a pension plan. Fewer and fewer companies have these, but many government workers still have them. Again, if this number is reported as a monthly payment, you'll have to multiply that number by 12 and enter the result in the calculator. This line also contains room for both spouses. Finally, I included a generic "Outside Income" line. As before, you'll need to annualize the total outside income by multiplying any monthly data by 12. You're now ready to proceed to the part everyone's been waiting almost 160 pages to do.

Here you go. The last section of the calculator contains one simple data output — your Goal-Oriented Target (your "number" from the title *Hey! What's my Number?*) Once all the above data is entered, just hit the "Press to Calculate" button. It's a big button. You can't miss it.

After everything has been entered in the data fields provided, you'll want to touch the "Press to Calculate" button and watch what number appears next to "Goal-Oriented Target ➜ (Your "Number")."

I'd like to comment on one question many financial planners might ask at this point: What about inflation? If you notice, this calculator does not account for inflation. There are several reasons for this. First, any across-the-board inflation assumption would be iffy at best. Second, as alluded to in the book *Your Money or Your Life*, (Joe Dominguez and Vicki Robin, Penguin Books, 1993), retirees often find adequate substitutes to escape the price increases measured by inflation indices. Third, as you'll see in the last chapter, you should review your retirement readiness at least yearly. These annual reviews automatically take into consideration the impacts (if any) of inflation through rising salaries, rising contribution rates, and rising required income objectives. Finally, as Andrew Carrillo says in Chapter Twenty-Seven, you can simply add your inflation assumption to your GOT to get an inflation-adjusted GOT. I don't recommend this because it's not based on real numbers (it is, after all, an assumption) and may generate misleading results. Better to just diligently update things on an annual basis and let nature take its course.

Great! You now have your own personal "Number" for retirement. How do you know it's good and what can you do about it if it's not good? Answers to these questions help you craft a plan that improves the odds you'll retire in comfort. You'll discover these answers next.

CHAPTER THIRTY-ONE:
IS YOUR RETIREMENT IN "PERIL"?
HOW TO ASSESS YOUR PERSONAL GOT

Yippee! Long hidden but always within reach, you've at last uncovered your number. Is your GOT 20%? Or is it 5%? Maybe you're one of the few who have obtained a GOT of 0%? What does it all mean? Is it good? Is it bad? Is your retirement in "Peril"? Or are you on the path to a comfortable retirement? How can you tell? And what do you do about it if you don't like what you've discovered? The next two chapters offer solutions to these questions

Table 2 below might be a useful way to begin to answer this question. The columns represent the number of years until you retire and the rows represent your GOT. Find the row and column that come closest to your personal numbers and look at the cell in the table where they intersect. For example, if you will retire in 10 years and your GOT is 3%, then the cell where they meet contains the figure "87.34%." What precisely does this 87.34% mean?

Table 2. How Good is My GOT?

GOT:	Years to Retirement: 1-Year	3-Year	5-Year	10-Year	15-Year	20-Year	25-Year	30-Year	35-Year	40-Year	45-Year	50-year
1%	71.59%	80.23%	80.95%	92.41%	97.30%	98.55%	98.44%	98.31%	98.15%	97.96%	97.73%	97.44%
2%	70.45%	79.07%	78.57%	88.61%	95.95%	98.55%	98.44%	98.31%	98.15%	97.96%	97.73%	97.44%
3%	69.32%	77.91%	77.38%	87.34%	93.24%	98.55%	98.44%	98.31%	98.15%	97.96%	97.73%	97.44%
4%	68.18%	76.74%	72.62%	83.54%	93.24%	97.10%	98.44%	98.31%	98.15%	97.96%	97.73%	97.44%
5%	67.05%	75.58%	67.86%	82.28%	87.84%	94.20%	98.44%	98.31%	98.15%	97.96%	97.73%	97.44%
6%	62.50%	69.77%	66.67%	77.22%	83.78%	94.20%	96.88%	98.31%	98.15%	97.96%	97.73%	97.44%
7%	59.09%	68.60%	65.48%	72.15%	72.97%	86.96%	96.88%	98.31%	98.15%	97.96%	97.73%	97.44%
8%	57.95%	62.79%	63.10%	63.29%	68.92%	78.26%	92.19%	98.31%	98.15%	97.96%	95.45%	94.87%
9%	57.95%	59.30%	57.14%	58.23%	59.46%	66.67%	82.81%	94.92%	96.30%	91.84%	90.91%	87.18%
10%	57.95%	55.81%	54.76%	48.10%	56.76%	60.87%	65.63%	83.05%	88.89%	71.43%	68.18%	66.67%
11%	55.68%	50.00%	46.43%	45.57%	47.30%	57.97%	50.00%	44.07%	50.00%	40.82%	36.36%	46.15%
12%	52.27%	48.84%	46.43%	43.04%	41.89%	42.03%	43.75%	33.90%	14.81%	12.24%	27.27%	23.08%
13%	51.14%	41.86%	42.86%	37.97%	36.49%	33.33%	28.13%	13.56%	1.85%	0.00%	2.27%	7.69%
14%	51.14%	39.53%	38.10%	34.18%	29.73%	23.19%	10.94%	0.00%	0.00%	0.00%	0.00%	0.00%
15%	50.00%	33.72%	27.38%	26.58%	24.32%	11.59%	3.13%	0.00%	0.00%	0.00%	0.00%	0.00%

Source: Ibbotson

I've strung together all the stock returns from 1926 through 2013 (data courtesy of Ibbotson Associates, a division of Morningstar and a leading provider of historical market return data). From that data, I've calculated every rolling period return from 1 rolling year to 70 rolling years. I've only shown the rolling year results for some years due to space limitations. Check out the web pages listed in the Afterword of this book for a greater array of charts like this one. (Heck, if I sell enough books I'll even be able to hire a programmer to automate these charts and link them to the Retirement Readiness Calculator.)

But enough about me. What about that "87.34%"?

That 87.34% means that for all rolling 10 year periods, (10 years being the number of years until retirement), the investment return met or exceeded the GOT of 3% a grand total of 87.34% of the time. That's a pretty good batting percentage and one that most people can live comfortably with. You might think of this number as the "Frequency," as in "How frequently the actual results for this period meet or exceed the GOT." This "Frequency" number is one way to measure the extent of any "Peril" you may be in.

For example, let's consider someone who will retire 40 years from now and has a GOT of 14%. We see where the lines intersect and we find a big fat goose egg of 0.00%. That's bad. It means in the last 88 years, there are no 40 year periods of stock market returns that yielded an annual return of at least 14%. This person stands to suffer a catastrophe when he misses his retirement. He is in great "Peril" and will definitely want to read the next chapter to find out how to lower his GOT. So, is there any range of GOTs that make a good target?

If you haven't figured it out by now, the lighter the shading on the table, the better off you are. Black is bad — it means there's been no period in recent history where stocks produced returns needed to match that GOT. In fact, I would venture to say anything where the figures themselves are in white (that's where the table is either black or dark gray) should be considered bad. In all these cases, the Frequency (i.e., the chances of meeting or exceeding your GOT) is less than 50%. By now, you'll understand when I say those folks with GOTs and years to retirement equating to a white number might be in "Peril" — i.e., a very dangerous situation when it comes to retiring in comfort.

Obviously, black numbers on a white background is best, but I would say anything in a light gray background is acceptable. Since many people have at least 15 years to go before they retire, this means any GOT at or below 6% is an acceptable number.

Let me say one thing about the average stock market return over this entire period. It's a little more than 10% and I've italicized the row where the GOT is equal to 10%. Many people (even professionals) like to use this 10% return number to project returns. As you can see from Table 2, a 10% GOT is only acceptable for people retiring in 30-35 years. Those are the only periods where the Frequency is greater than 80%. That's why I used the 8% number in the forward-looking return calculations in this book. It has a higher degree of likelihood of actually being achieved, including all periods extending beyond 25 years.

A Special Word for Those Whose GOT is "0%"

No, you didn't break the calculator. A "0%" GOT means you are on course to accumulate the assets you need to achieve a comfortable retirement without getting any return on those assets. It means you don't have to take any risk at all. Does that mean you shouldn't invest? I'll leave that for you to decide for yourself or with the help of a professional adviser.

In the meantime, for those of you who are well within the lighter shades of Table 2, (in other words, for the most part those with a GOT of 6% or less), I say, "Congratulations! You have an acceptable GOT." Your level of "Peril" is very small. For those who want to improve their GOT, I've got some ideas for you in the next chapter.

Hmm. Come to think of it, even if you're in the lighter shades, you might want to go over some of the tricks outlined in the ensuing pages. Why? You'll find out in, oh, about the second paragraph. (What? Did someone just say Monty Python?")

In either situation, it's likely this whole "GOT" thing is something you're unaccustomed to. If you're normal, this lack of familiarity might create anxiety. And I have no doubt the higher your GOT is, the higher this anxiety level will be. In which case, here are a handful of useful tips for you...

CHAPTER THIRTY-TWO:
5 THINGS TO DO TO IMPROVE YOUR GOT

F irst and foremost, don't panic. You have plenty of options before you. Most of them are OK, but all of them might require some discipline on your part. My guess is, though, if you've made it this far into the book, you're pretty astute and already have some idea of what you can do. In fact, I bet you've already played around with your *Hey! What's My Number?* Retirement Readiness Calculator and plugged in a lot of different numbers. Extra bonus points for you! That's exactly why I designed this tool. It's not meant to provide a rock solid never-changing piece of advice. It's meant to change as you change, evolve as you evolve, and grow as you grow.

While this might sound promising to someone who currently has a GOT they're *not* comfortable with, it should also be viewed as a warning to those who think they *are* satisfied with the personal GOT they've just calculated. Why? You can change your behavior to improve your GOT (and the odds you'll retire in comfort). You can also change your behavior — whether purposefully or not — that can harm your GOT (and the odds you'll retire in comfort). And it's not all on you (either way). Remember the "Nobody Expects the Spanish Inquisition" Rule? Random events occur throughout our lives that either bless us or injure us. In both cases, annually recalculating your GOT is a necessity.

So the GOT is not a static number. In this chapter, though, I want to concentrate on the second most habitually asked question I receive: "What can I do to improve my GOT?" (Recall, the most asked question is: *Hey! What's My Number?*) The answers are more straightforward than you might suspect. And you can use the *Hey! What's My Number?* Retirement Readiness Calculator to see how these solutions can help you. I'll review these solutions based on what I've seen most people do first.

1. **Increase your annual contribution.** As I wrote earlier, most financial advisers suggest aiming for a goal of contributing between 15%-20% of your salary into your retirement plan. Experiment with the Retirement Readiness Calculator on this. You'll be amazed how much difference this can have, especially

if you have several decades before you retire. Think back to our hypothetical 28 year old from Chapter Twenty-Eight. He had a GOT of 6.17% without including Social Security and a GOT of 2.97% with Social Security. Let's say he wanted to keep a GOT of 3% and still save enough to not depend on Social Security. He could accomplish this by increasing his annual contribution rate from 3% to 15%.

2. **Lower your projected retirement income.** The 80% Rule is just a guess. You can actually determine your true retirement expenses with greater accuracy as you get closer to retirement. Most people usually try to cut their retirement expense to get a lower GOT. I don't recommend it. It's way too risky and often filled with overly optimistic assumptions. Nonetheless, this is number two on the most-likely-to-try list. If our 28 year-old wanted to retain the 3% GOT without relying on Social Security and without raising contributions, he would need to cut expenses from $50,000 a year to $19,000 a year. You see, that's not a very realistic expectation. Don't try to lower your GOT by reducing your projected retirement income.

3. **Work Longer (full-time at the same company).** Some people simply resign themselves to never retiring and assume their current employer will have no problem with this. For a few people this assumption is reasonable, for many others it's a pipedream. If our 28 year-old wants to retain the 3% GOT without relying on Social Security, without increasing contributions, and without reducing retirement expenses, he would have to work at his current employer another 27 years beyond his originally intended retirement date. Yeah. Sure.

4. **Work Longer (part-time).** This generally proves more difficult than expected. You can pick one of your hobbies that offers an opportunity to earn extra cash or you can work at retail outlets who are always seeking veteran (read "more reliable") associates. Of course, for our 28 year old looking to ditch Social Security and still retain that 3% GOT without doing anything, all he needs to do is to find a job that replaces the Social Security annual payment of $31,092. Hmm, maybe that's not as easy as it sounds.

5. **Some Combination of All of the Above.** Eventually, people surrender to the idea that there is no "sure-fire" easy way to reduce their GOT. So, they try some combination of all of

them. A reasonable combination for our 28 year old is: Increase savings to 10% and find a part-time post-retirement job that pays $13,000 a year. Do that, and earn 3% a year means this fellow won't be relying on Social Security. Now, this combination choice seems much more reasonable than some of the single options above, doesn't it?

Remember, the best way to get to where you want to go is to create a plan. If you run through a number of scenarios, you should have enough information to finalize your plan. You should know what your target saving percentage (or "salary deferral rate") should be, when you should expect to retire, and, very roughly, what you anticipate spending in retirement. If you don't have these numbers yet, rerun the calculator.

Finally, the most important thing to remember is time heals all wounds. The more time you have, the more options you have, and the easier it is to lower your GOT. It's also vital to take a balanced approach on this. If you've got 20 years until you retire and a GOT of 5%, don't knock yourself out trying to lower it to 3% "just because." It makes no sense to starve yourself today so you can live lavishly for a tomorrow that may never come. On the flip-side, we have the lesson from the same hedonistic "eat, drink, and be merry for tomorrow we shall die" approach a lot of baby boomers took in the 1980s. Those that survived are regretting it.

We'll end with this little ditty from Aristotle: "The virtue of justice consists in moderation, as regulated by wisdom." Or, if you prefer the Latin to the Greek, there's Cicero who said, "Never go to excess, but let moderation be your guide."

Whether Greek or Roman, the philosophy was as true then as it is now. The best practice is to balance the needs of today with the needs of tomorrow. Sometimes that means living in moderation.

*   *   *   *   *

Congratulations. You've finished the book. There's only one more thing left to do...

AFTERWORD:
WHAT TO DO WHEN YOU'RE DONE
READING THIS BOOK

Hey! *What's My Number?* is not the kind of book you only read once then throw away, give away, or sell at the annual family garage sale. No, *Hey! What's My Number?* is a book you need to re-read once a year. It's designed that way because that's the way the real world of retirement savings works.

You can never predict the future, so an annual update of the material covered in Section V is required. You may or may not have any specific changes in your personal life, but your underlying numbers will change as you earn more money and save more money. In addition, investments will have an impact on your retirement savings (hopefully positive, but every so often negative). This is why everything needs to be updated once a year.

More important, unless you have some brand new circumstances or changes in your life, this update should occur ONLY once a year. Building a nest egg for retirement is a marathon, not a sprint. Checking your status too frequently may (and often does) lead to the kind of errors we discussed in Section III.

Since by now I'm sure you're waiting for the muscle car analogy, picture this annual update in the same way you'd give your car an annual inspection. In that sense, the *Hey! What's My Number?* Retirement Readiness Calculator is like a "Check Engine" light. It will signal to you if there's a problem with your retirement vehicle(s). It's designed simply enough for those of you who like to pop open the hood and test things yourself. It also works for those who prefer to hire a financial "mechanic" to help tune-up their retirement engine. In both cases, the Calculator allows you to investigate different scenarios using the data variables you can enter into it. As the previous chapter shows, you can change the data one variable at a time or all at once.

The above notwithstanding, I would greatly encourage you to share this book with your family, friends, and associates. But don't give them your copy. Remember, you'll need it as both an annual booster shot and as a way to keep your personal data updated. This may sound like a conundrum, but there are alternatives.

Here's what I will shamelessly suggest:

1) Do you have someone in your family who really likes *Hey! What's My Number?* Then buy my book for them as a gift.

2) Does one of your friends really like *Hey! What's My Number?* and do you like that person? Then buy my book for them as a gift.

3) Does one of your friends really like *Hey! What's My Number?* but you don't like that person? Then tell them to buy their own copy.

4) Does one of your coworkers like *Hey! What's My Number?* Then just tell your company to buy a copy of my book for every employee.

Seriously, though, if you find this book helpful and you want to seek more information along a similar vein, then you might be interested in the following websites:

If you're an individual retirement saver, then you might find my site *LifetimeDreamGuide.com* to your liking. We all desire to know the meaning of our life. *LifetimeDreamGuide.com* provides, for the first time in written form, a proven method that can now help you achieve your lifetime dream. Learn how the lessons of such greats as Socrates, Aristotle and Thomas Jefferson can show you how to make your own personal path as you pursue happiness in any kind of economic environment. You can sign up for this site's newsletter and get prompted on the latest tricks, ideas, and success stories for those looking to achieve their own personal lifetime dream. You also have free access to the *Hey! What's My Number?* Retirement Readiness Calculator

If you're a plan sponsor, service provider, or government regulator, look into my site *FiduciaryNews.com*. *FiduciaryNews.com* provides essential information, blunt commentary, and practical examples for ERISA/401k fiduciaries, individual trustees, and professional fiduciaries. This site features a newsletter geared especially for this audience. It is also a gateway to *FiduciaryNews.net*, a peer-to-peer community that provides premium content not available to the public, including the *Hey! What's My Number?* Retirement Readiness Calculator and more tools associated with those described in this book.

Now, go get started on achieving that retirement dream you've always been dreaming of…

SECTION SIX:

– APPENDICES –

*THE SECTION OF THE BOOK
YOU'LL MOST LIKELY BOOKMARK*

APPENDIX I.
8 BASIC INVESTMENT CONCEPTS EVERY 401K SAVER MUST UNDERSTAND

The evidence overwhelmingly indicates most employees have a problem saving. That's why focusing their attention on savings is critical to their achieving retirement success. There are those few, however, who are well on their way to saving enough and who have the time, resources, and interest to devote to learning the art of investing. These folks generally belong in the "Do-it-Yourself" category of a tiered fund option menu.

With that in mind, we polled several prominent investment advisers and asked them to identify the most important investing concepts 401k participants should understand. Here are the top eight:

What is a Mutual Fund? Nearly every 401k plan is comprised of mutual funds. When you buy shares in a mutual fund, you're buying into a pool of securities, for example, chosen and managed by a professional portfolio manager. Of all the other types of funds that also bring together assets from different people into one portfolio (e.g., common trust funds, hedge funds, etc.) this is the most highly-regulated. A mutual fund buys individual securities, such as stocks and bonds, and a professional portfolio manager is responsible for monitoring and managing these investments. Most mutual funds invest only in stocks, some only in bonds, and a growing number invest in both. Mutual funds are generally considered diversified investments, although some may specialize in single industry sectors.

The Risk-Return Relationship: The "Soundbite of the Century," courtesy of Harry Markowitz and what eventually became known as "Modern Portfolio Theory" states "risk and return are related." As you take on more risk, you increase your odds of scoring big gains. Of course, there's a flipside to this many would prefer to ignore. "Investors often assume that taking more risk means you will make more money. This is not always true," says Amy Rose Herrick. Herrick continues, "What this does mean is that your account values may swing up and down more than with a lower risk, stable value option. Those swings will work for or against you depending on when you plan to retire or when you will start spending the money accumulated in those assets. Investors in 2000-2002 and again in 2008-2009 were horrified that investments that had been performing so well dropped as much as 30-50% quickly. Many of them erroneously thought that being labeled a 'moderate conservative model' meant that kind of loss 'couldn't happen to me' — it did."

In the end, though, there is no "one right answer." How each individual manages the risk-return relationship will be up to that individual. "Know yourself and manage risk appropriately. It's important to get your mix right, especially early, because mistakes can have long-lasting effects," says Gary Pattengale, a Wealth Manager for Balasa Dinverno Foltz LLC in Itasca, Illinois.

Diversification: In one of the greatest ironies of modern investing, advisers often misquote Mark Twain as saying "don't keep all your eggs in one basket." In fact, he said just the opposite. He said "Keep all your eggs in one basket and watch that basket!" In other words, we can't ignore the costs of diversification. Ol' Samuel Clemens was advising us not to overextend our resources and just to simply stick to what we know. Still, the concept of diversification is important. "The market is fickle, and the most successful way to deal with that is to spread your risk. If one category is not performing well, only a portion of your portfolio is impacted, rather than the entire account," says Ozeme Bonnette.

Still, don't lose sight of Twain's adage. Lauren G. Lindsay, Director of Financial Planning at Personal Financial Advisors in Covington, Louisiana, says, "Diversify appropriate to YOU. Just because the guy next to you is doing it, doesn't mean it is right for you. Most plans now include some kind of risk test, and it's a good idea to take it. And age is not an indicator of risk. We have ultra-conservative 20 year olds and super-aggressive 70 year olds so things tied to age are not always appropriate."

Asset Allocation: "Asset allocation means how much money you will have allocated to each type of investment," says Thomas Batterman, Principal at Financial Fiduciaries/Vigil Trust & Financial Advocacy in Wausau, Wisconsin. "So for example, if we look just at the broad categories of stocks and bonds and define stocks as risky and bonds as safe, what percentage should you have in stocks and what percentage should you have in bonds? It can and should go further than that. As you have more money to invest you might get into suballocations within your stock investments. These can include allocations to 'safer' stock investments versus more 'risky' stock asset classes. But at the end of the day it is about how much you will invest in each asset class. There are again numerous online resources to assist with education on this point. In the way we work, clients hire us to do this kind of stuff for them because they don't understand much about it and don't want to take the time to learn."

Christopher Long, President of Long Financial Planning in Chicago, Illinois, says, "Investors can develop an asset allocation that best fits their time horizon (younger=more risk, older=less risk), tolerance for short-term decline (take 50% of the stock allocation to determine the potential short-term loss e.g. 50% stock means a 25% potential short-term loss), and long-term growth rate. (Stocks have averaged 9-10% over the long-term, bonds 5-6%)."

Time is on Your Side: Elle Kaplan, says, "The beauty of investing lies in the ability of your wealth to grow over a long period of time. The short-term market 'noise' is not what matters. With a sound investing strategy and a well-diversified portfolio, there is no need to follow the day-to-day ups and downs." Long adds, "Often 401k plan participants save too little or do not invest in their 401k plan because they think they can 'catch up' later when they will be able to save more. This is especially true of young investors. They do not realize that for each 8–9 years they wait to start investing the amount they need to invest doubles. (e.g. if they needed to save 5% of their income at age 22, they will need to save 10% if they start at age 30, and 20% if they start at age 38)."

Don't Time the Market: Here's a classic problem that lures many naïve investors into its trap with the promise of riches. Unsuspecting 401k investors "chase performance and buy whatever was up the most last year. Then, when it goes down, they sell it and buy the next best performer, and so on. It's a losing game," says Pattengale, who further warns, "Don't engage in dangerous market timing. Very few can do it successfully especially over long periods. The best chance to succeed is by picking an allocation you can stick with in any market environment."

Bonnette says, "Timing the market means trying to keep up with what is 'hot' and moving funds from one opportunity to the next, hoping to maximize returns. It is important not to time the market because the majority of investors who chase 'hot' ideas usually perform worse than those who create a well-diversified portfolio. Most often, by the time the news reaches the masses, the biggest part of the market run-up has already occurred, and it is too late to get maximum value. If the 'hot' market suddenly runs cold, the chances are greater for losing a lot before moving the money out. Ignore the desire to shuffle your portfolio every time the media reports 'breaking news.' Stick to your diversified portfolio!"

Pay Attention to Fees that Matter: There's a lot of talk about fees since the Department of Labor required service providers to fully disclose fees. Noah Greenbaum, Director of Portfolio Management at Canal Capital Management in Richmond, Virginia, says, "Many investment and insurance companies load up participant fund options with their own proprietary mutual funds because it helps pad their bottom line. So I would encourage every participant to research what proportion of the funds available on the platform are owned by the 401k offering company. This is important because we need to ensure that investors are getting objective advice. The ultimate goal of the 401k is to build a retirement nest egg for plan participants, not executives on Wall Street. I would also encourage participants to ask their employer to use a 401k platform company that does not even have proprietary investments, thus avoiding conflicts altogether."

Batterman says, "Costs inside mutual funds can make a huge difference in the long-term performance of your investments. It is important to take a look at the cost structures of funds you might use. Cheaper is not always better — if it were, K-mart would still be a thriving enterprise. But cost is a factor."

Fees are too important for them to only be mentioned here. See more on them in *Appendix III. Mutual Fund Fees that Really Matter.*

Monitor and Adjust as Needed: Unlike 401k investors who choose the "Do-it-For-Me" categories (i.e., those who want professionally managed portfolios and who will often choose just a single fund), those in the "Do-it-Yourself" category will need to spend more time monitoring their investments. Bonnette says, "Choosing a well-diversified portfolio is not a one-time thing. The investments should still be monitored regularly and adjusted when needed. If an investment is not performing well compared to comparable/similar opportunities, it may be time to shift. Rebalancing (adjusting asset allocations among the investment options) is also important to make sure that the portfolio does not become less diversified due to market performance. An investment option that is good today may not be good forever. Managers change, company dynamics change, etc. It is important to stay invested, but that doesn't have to mean staying in the exact same investments forever. When other, better options are available, it will make for a stronger portfolio outcome. Monitor your investment options when the statements arrive. Monitor the other options available. Be willing to switch to comparable/similar options if what you're holding is no longer doing well."

What all these basic concepts come down to is focusing on processes over outcomes. Michael T. McKeown, says, "Investors cannot control the outcomes of the markets, but they can control the investment process. This is important because behaviorally, our feeble human brains often want to change course when our portfolios run into turbulence. If we can harness our emotions and stick to the process laid out from the beginning, investors can be buyers from others that may be liquidating at inopportune times, of they can be selling to uneconomic buyers."

APPENDIX II.
A TRIP DOWN MEMORY LANE –
REVISITING PORTFOLIO OPTIMIZATION

L et's get one thing straight from the start: This is about unsystematic risk, not systematic risk. Systematic risk affects all investments. Diversification does not address systematic risk.

Unsystematic risk is limited to very specific investments. That's why they also call it "specific" risk. You can diversify away unsystematic risk. And that's precisely what a fellow by the name of Harry Markowitz began toying with before Elvis Presley even graduated high school. Today we call it "portfolio optimization," but in 1952, Markowitz titled his Journal of Finance (7,1) paper "Portfolio Selection."

By 1959, the father of Modern Portfolio Theory had refined his description when he published his book *Portfolio Selection: Efficient Diversification of Investments* (Wiley, New York). Those interested might note in those seven years, the crooner from Tupelo had become pretty efficient himself, with a diversified portfolio of an even dozen (including eleven in a row) chart-topping #1 hit songs on the Billboard Hot 100. Markowitz had been just as prolific, if only in the rarified air of finance, and not yet quite as famous. More importantly, he had come up with the beginnings of a quantifiably-based approach to reducing "risk" in a portfolio. In effect, he had figured out a way to scientifically prove what the court had intimated in *Harvard College v. Amory* some 150 years earlier — adding more stocks in a portfolio could diversify a substantial amount of the risk.

From that point, the race was on. Who would be the first to answer the question "What's the fewest number of stocks a portfolio should optimally hold?" Anyone taking an advanced degree program in economics might smile at the question as the mathematical elegance of those portfolio optimization formulae foisted upon them by a force of finance professors bubbles up within their rosy memories. Let's take a trip down memory lane and recall some of the highlights of portfolio optimization and how it influenced our thoughts on diversification.

The next notable step in the search for the optimal portfolio size occurred in 1968 with the publication of "Diversification and the

Reduction of Dispersion: an Empirical Analysis" by J.L. Evans and S.H. Archer in the *Journal of Finance* (23, 761-767). The two researchers looked at several randomly-selected portfolios and tried to determine how much risk was reduced based on the number of stocks held. They concluded 10 randomly selected stocks can, for all intents and purposes, achieve sufficient diversification. This development immediately questioned the economic justification of any portfolio consisting of more than 10 stocks. Needless to say, this rocked the small world of portfolio managers that then existed on their daily ration of the Nifty Fifty.

Two years later, L. Fisher and J.H. Lorie published "Some Studies of Variability of Returns on Investments in Common Stocks" in the *Journal of Business* (43 (1970), 99-134). This duo lent further support to the thesis developed by Evans and Archer. Fisher and Lorie created simulated results for a broad array of portfolio sizes using every stock listed on the New York Stock Exchange. By looking at the return distributions for the years between 1926 and 1965, they showed one could diversify away the unsystematic risk by 80% using a portfolio of just eight stocks.

By now the go-go 60's had begun to melt down into the stagnant 70's, and the prominence of the Blue Chips faded to black with the rise of the small caps (multiple year recessions tend to do that). A new breed of renegades left the stultifying trust departments and brokerage firms, creating a slew of registered investment advisers. They more aggressively pursued the previously neglected smaller companies as the no-longer-Nifty Fifty wallowed in infamy.

Within the walls of ivy, a different kind of newness had taken hold. A growing number of published pieces began speaking of "the market" as if it could be a portfolio. Portfolio optimization, in a sense, became a loser's game, with the only pure diversification consisting of market-sized portfolios. Of course, the business schoolmarms would insist an "index" portfolio represented a mere theoretical construct and could not be created in the real world. But by mid-decade, a non-conformist from Valley Forge, Pennsylvania named John Bogle had birthed his baby proving the folly of those professorial disclaimers.

But, could such a large portfolio really achieve optimal diversification, even in theory? In the year marking the death of Elvis Presley, along came E.J. Elton and M.J. Gruber with their paper entitled "Risk Reduction and Portfolio Size: an Analytical Solution" (*Journal of Business*, 50 (1977), 415-437). Rather than continuing on the road paved by Evans and Archer, these two went back to Markowitz. Elton and Gruber then developed a precise quantitative formula relating risk to the number of holdings in a portfolio. They then used that device to attack the work of Evan and Archer as well as Fisher and Lorie. Implying the prevailing consensus suggesting optimal diversification would be achieved with only 10 or 20 stocks, Elton and Gruber concluded risk can be significantly reduced when one increases the size of the portfolio from 15 to 100 stocks.

But the pressure of real world dynamics could not be ignored, not even by academia. J. Mayshar, with his publication of "Transaction Cost in a Model of Capital Market Equilibrium" in the *Journal of Political Economy* (87 (1979), 673-700), was the first to point out the problems association with overdiversification. Mayshar, repeating the practical constraints of the business school professors, cited practical considerations would mute any perceived benefits of supposed diversification of portfolios with a large number of holdings. Specifically, he argued increasing transaction costs hurt more than any good derived from diversification. He then presented an "equilibrium model," showing, in light of transaction costs, a portfolio is optimized when it limits the number of stocks it holds.

Mayshar's research nipped Elton and Gruber in the bud, and later studies returned to the issue of trying to determine how many stocks the optimally diverse portfolio should hold. In 1982, T. Tole's paper "You Can't Diversify Without Diversifying" appeared in the *Journal of Portfolio Management*, (8, 5-11). Tole conducted his research using a method employing R^2 (a standard statistical construct that only statisticians — and portfolio managers — care about) rather than the usual averaging technique. He concluded optimal diversification occurred in a portfolio consisting of 25-40 stocks.

In 1987, the appropriately named M. Statman published the seminal paper on this subject, coincidentally entitled "How Many Stocks Make a Diversified Portfolio?" (*Journal of Financial and Quantitative Analysis*, 22 (1987), 353-363). He concluded that a well-diversified portfolio should optimally hold between 30-40 stocks. Needless to say this became fodder for the standard MBA curriculum from the late 1980's. But, lest you think it's outdated, you should note well that the 2010 CFA Study Guide still highlights this particular piece of research.

Statman's work seems to have exhausted any further new discoveries in this line of research. Most of the ensuing studies appear to merely confirm Statman, albeit using foreign market data. Huck Khoon Chung's 2000 Ph.D. thesis for Universiti Sains Malaysia: "How Many Securities Make a Well-Diversified Portfolio: KLSE Stocks." The thesis was based on the data of Malaysian stocks from 1988-1997. It used the Statman technique and the Markowitz model in its analysis. Under Statman, the optimal portfolio contained 27 stocks. Using the Markowitz model, the optimal portfolio contained 22 stocks.

Most recently, F. S. Al Suqaier and H. A. Al Ziyud, ("The Effect of Diversification on Achieving Optimal Portfolio," *European Journal of Economics, Finance and Administrative Sciences*, 32 (2011)) likewise looked at data from the Amman Stock Exchange (ASE) over the period 2/12/2005 to 3/3/2010. They concluded "that (43%) of the total risk could be eliminated by holding (2) stocks portfolio, and holding only (3) stocks portfolio could reduce half of the total risk. As we hold (15) stocks portfolio, investors can reduce (92%) of the total risk, and to eliminate (96%) of the total risk investors need to hold (25) stocks portfolio finally, (55) stocks portfolio to eliminate (99%) of the total risk reduction obtained through diversification. In addition, holding (15-16) stocks are required to capture most of the benefits associated with diversification."

After more than a half century of research, academia seems to have settled upon a range defining the limits of the usefulness of diversification regarding the number of stocks in a portfolio. This range appears to be from 15-50 stocks with the most likely optimal amount between 30 and 40 stocks. Beyond that, the cost of diversification both in terms of out-of-pocket expenses and the risk/return tradeoff start to eat into a portfolio's performance.

Ironically, just as this process began, The King sang us the ultimate advice. On January 4, 1956, Elvis released the single "Too Much." Two days later he performed it on the Ed Sullivan Show. It would reach #1 on the Billboard chart. If we only knew then what we know today...

Appendix III.
Mutual Fund Fees that Really Matter

Have you ever gone to a dealer to buy a car? If so, you've probably heard about this thing called "dealer cost." That's how much the dealer paid the car company for the car. Anything above that represents the "dealer mark-up." When you negotiate with the dealer, the only thing you're negotiating is how high the dealer mark-up will be. Because you understand no dealer will sell the car for less than what he bought it for, as a buyer, you're goal is to pay the dealer cost.

Or is it? Do you think the dealer will stay in business long if he continually fails to make any money selling cars? Absolutely not! And, as a buyer, do you want the dealer you just spent a bunch of buck to buy a car from to go out of business? Absolutely not! No, you want him to stay in business for at least as long as you own the car, mostly because you want to nag him for any service warranty and similar such things.

I think a lot of people instinctively understand this about buying cars. They don't expect to pay less than dealer cost and they do expect to pay a reasonable dealer markup (for which they're more than comfortable dickering with the dealer on). What surprises me, then, is why people — and here I include both journalists and investors — don't make the same connection with financial services, and, in particular, mutual funds.

Chapter Eighteen already showed you the folly of looking at mutual fund expense ratios as a proxy for performance (with the important exception of index funds). In many ways, the mutual fund expense ratio is like the dealer cost. It represents the cost of running the business of the mutual fund. Many of these costs are mandated by the government for the safety of investors. In fact, you can buy less expensive collective funds from banks (conveniently called, "bank collective funds" or "common trust funds"), but they don't have the same mandated safeguards the government places on mutual funds. (There's a reason for this. In the 1930s, many felt these bank collective funds lead to the financial crisis that caused the 1929 stock market crash and the Great Depression. As such, with the sole allowance in the case of bank trust clients, they were effectively outlawed and replaced by "Registered Investment Companies" (or "mutual funds" in the common parlance).

If the expense ratio is to mutual funds in the same way the dealer cost is to cars, what do they really mean? D. Bruce Johnsen, a professor at George Mason University School of Law, discusses this in his study "Myths About Mutual Fund Fees: Economic Insights on Jones v. Harris" (George Mason School of Law, Law & Economics Research Paper No. 09-49, posted October 7, 2009). He likes to explain his findings by retelling a story from his youth.

Like many college students, Johnsen faced a summertime dilemma. Painting houses to earn money for school, a homeowner called him to do a difficult job. Johnsen looked at the house and realized it required stain — something he had never done before. He really needed the money, so he offered to do the job for $300. The owner looked at the young college student and frowned. Johnsen's heart sank. But the customer countered, "How about if I pay you $450?" The incredulous scholar absentmindedly asked, "Why? That's more than what I'm asking for." The wily owner only smiled and replied, "Sure, but I want you to do a good job."

Johnsen never forgot that story. The common sense "you get what you pay for" philosophy permeates his paper. He explains, "Although you wouldn't know this from reading the popular press, economic theory clearly suggests paying high fees is justified in a world where the average shareholder doesn't have the wherewithal to monitor the adviser to assess the quality of services. This is known as the efficiency wage notion. In other words, reducing fees entails an added cost that can be more than the savings... To assume high fees reduce returns dollar-for-dollar is simply wrong. Lower fees are not necessarily better where you cannot observe quality."

If the mutual fund expense ratio doesn't matter, then what mutual fund fees do matter? For that, we have several studies that provide compelling reasons why certain fees associated with mutual funds, specifically, mutual fund sales, do matter.

The working paper, "Broker Incentives and Mutual Fund Market Segmentation," (NEBR, August 2010), was written by Diane Del Guercio (Lundquist College of Business), Jonahan Reuter (Carroll School of Management at Boston College) and Paula A. Tkac (Federal Reserve Bank of Atlanta). I spoke with Jon Reuter, Assistant Professor of Finance in the Carroll School of Management at Boston College who explained the primary purpose of the paper was to try to uncover an economic purpose for the use of certain distribution models within the mutual fund industry. The researchers found "robust evidence that funds distributed through the direct channel outperform comparable funds distributed through other channels by 1% per year."

Professor Reuter pointed out their paper "extended the analysis (along several dimensions)" of a 2009 study "Assessing the Costs and Benefits of Brokers in the Mutual Fund Industry," by Daniel Bergstresser (Harvard Business School), John M. R. Chalmers (Lundquist College of Business, University of Oregon) and Peter Tufano (Harvard Business School and NBER) published May 21, 2009 in *The Review of Financial Studies*. Reuter credits this study as the first to "document before-fee performance differences between direct-sold and broker-sold funds." The NEBR paper confirms these results and then some.

The 2009 study, however, did not include institutional funds in its analysis. Reuter's paper does – and that can have far reaching implications to retirement savers. In a nutshell, the paper concludes direct-sold mutual funds (including institutional funds) outperform broker-sold mutual funds by 1%. Professor Reuter agrees "it is reasonable to conclude" 401k plan sponsors – and the participants of their plans – on average will tend to benefit avoiding funds with sales charges.

The paper, "It Pays to Set the Menu: Mutual Fund Investment Options in 401k Plans," (Pool, Veronika Krepely, Sialm, Clemens and Stefanescu, Irina, January 20, 2013), is the result of work done by researchers from Indiana University and the University of Texas at Austin. . Pool et al concluded trustees with a conflict of interest are more likely than unconflicted trustees to keep and to add poorer performing affiliated funds. Worse, employees continued to invest in these poorer performing options even though they had better alternatives.

The study reveals something that stunned even the researchers. "Perhaps the most surprising result was the future underperformance for the lowest performance decile funds," says Stefanescu. The study concludes "We estimate that on average they underperform by approximately 3.6% annually on a risk-adjusted basis. This figure is large in and of itself, but its economic significance is magnified in the retirement context by compounding. Our results suggest that the trustee bias we document in this paper has important implications for the employees' income in retirement."

What is the magnitude of these "implications"? I did the calculations and this and wrote about it in an article titled, "Study: SEC Fiduciary Delay Costing Retirement Investors $1 Billion per Month," (*FiduciaryNews.com*, February 12, 2013).

What are these fees and how can you find them? Simply look on the second or third page. Under the heading "Risk/Return Summary: Fee Table," you'll see two sections are the very beginning. The first one is called "Shareholder Fees (fees paid directly from your investment)." These are various forms of commissions and transactions fees. In other words, these are the fees you pay for the "broker-sold" funds Reuter refers to. If these aren't listed as either "None" or "0.00%" you've got a problem. Find a new fund.

The second section is called "Annual Series' Operating Expenses (expenses that you pay each year as a percentage of the value of your investment)." This is normally the "dealer cost" portion of the fund, but not entirely. There is one line called "Distribution [and/or Service](12b-1) Fees." Again, this isn't a "cost of doing business" line item, it is another one of those "broker-sold" numbers. If this figure isn't either "None" or "0.00%" you've got a problem. Find a new fund.

There is one other category of "bad"fees, but it's a lot harder to find. It's so hard to find, even professionals have a hard time finding it. It's a very sneaky way for mutual funds to pay for distribution. It's called "revenue sharing" and it's not currently required to be easily disclosed in the mutual fund prospectus. The best you can do is ask your retirement plan sponsor or you're mutual fund company directly. Unfortunately, too many popular funds pay revenue sharing. The safest way to ensure you're not paying any revenue sharing fees is to purchase your shares directly from the fund company. Most people don't do this anymore (thirty years ago most people did do this), because they like the "convenience" of getting a custodian statement that contains all their funds, no matter what fund family they've been purchased for.

Do you think the average investor knows the true fee associated with this "convenience"?

Neither do I.

APPENDIX IV.
VOLATILITY AS RISK — WHERE IT ALL BEGAN AND WHY IT WENT WRONG

We need to get an idea of how the problem of defining risk as volatility started in the first place. It begins with a familiar phrase, one that launched the advent of Modern Portfolio Theory (MPT) in the 1950s: "Risk and Return are related." This is the common-sense relationship Harry Markowitz famously wrote of in his famous treatise "Portfolio Selection" (*Journal of Finance*, 1952) even before Bill Haley and the Comets took their turn rockin' around that clock of theirs. (Well, you didn't expect me to use the Elvis Presley reference again, did you? Besides, mentioning that particular Bill Haley song allows me to write…)

Oh, those were happier days back then, the greatest generation having just won World War Two, the same "good war" both Heller and Vonnegut would reference a generation later. The big theme of the Allies' success in the Second World War revolved around such words as "logistics" and "operations." Everything was reduced to numbers, and, with a basketball sized hunk of beeping metal about to thrust the world into the Sputnik Era, it didn't take much to transform portfolio management from a droll accounting exercise to a formula-laden scientific enterprise.

As we all know, formulas (or "formulae," for those who have been blessed with an education in the Latin language) contain, in addition to various mathematical operands, loads of numbers, and variables (variables being merely numbers in disguise as letters). Everyone could easily pick out the number we needed to use for "return," but folks had a devil of a time identifying the right number to use for "risk." Without a reliably quantifiable method, trying to assess risk was nothing more than hocus-pocus. Finally, Markowitz discovered the solution.

Alas, computers back then weren't powerful enough for him to use it, so he had to settle on something called "standard deviation." What is a standard deviation? The best way to explain this is show you a graph of what statisticians call a "Normal Distribution."

Graph 8. Normal Distribution

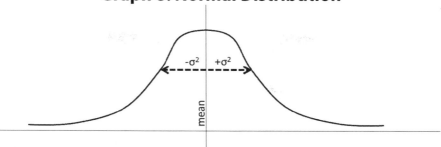

Source: Author

Normal distributions (this "Bell Curve" shape you see in Graph 8) don't occur often in real life. They require a lot of randomized data. It's rare to see a normal distribution in the investment world, especially for investment returns. But that's the least of our concerns. For now, let's be charitable to these wizards of Wall Street and agree, for the sake of argument, the data they are analyzing is normally distributed. In a normal distribution, you have this line smack dab in the middle of the whole thing. That's called the "mean." It represents the average of all the data. For example, if our data were all the numbers from 0 to 100, then 50 would represent the mean. (Don't confuse this with the "median." The median is the number that sits smack dab in the middle of a chronological list of numbers. Sometimes, the median and the mean are the same number, but that's not always the case. By coincidence — and by definition — in a normal distribution, the mean and the median are the same number.)

You might notice the squiggly thing in the middle of the graph. That's the Greek letter sigma (σ). It's one of those variables I told you about earlier. In this case, σ^2 represents one standard deviation. (For those purists, at least the ones that remember their statistics courses, σ represents what's called the "variance.") One standard deviation to the right of the mean ($+\sigma^2$) represents a third of all the data points in our normal distribution. Likewise, one standard deviation to the left of the mean ($-\sigma^2$) also represents (albeit a different one) a third of all the data points in our normal distribution. Together, two-thirds of all the data points lie within one standard deviation from the mean (that is, from $-\sigma^2$ to $+\sigma^2$). Standard deviation is therefore a measure of how much the data sample varies from the mean.

Why is this important? Because standard deviations come in different sizes based on the shape of the Bell Curve. Here's an example of several different Bell Curve shapes.

Graph 9. Different Normal Distribution Graphs

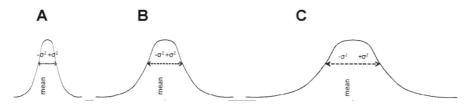

Source: Author

From the graph above, you can see the standard deviation of Bell Curve A is smaller than the standard deviation of Bell Curve B, which is smaller than the standard deviation of Bell Curve C. Another way of saying this is that Bell Curve C has more variability than Bell Curve B, which, in turn, has more variability than Bell Curve A. Now let's substitute the word "volatility" in place of "variability" since that's how finance professors define "volatility." We can therefore say Bell Curve C has the greatest volatility and Bell Curve A has the least volatility.

It is this volatility that first Markowitz and then others used to define risk. Right off the bat, you can see why Markowitz only wanted to use only the $-\sigma^2$ portion of the standard deviation and not the $+\sigma^2$. Using only the $-\sigma^2$ portion is called the "semi-variance" and, in layman's terms, measures only that portion of the data that falls below the mean. This is important because, for Markowitz, the mean represented the expected return. The $+\sigma^2$ portion of the standard deviation measures what falls above the mean. Again, in Markowitz terms, that means the data that exceeds the expected return. Markowitz preferred to isolate only that portion of returns that missed the expected return, but, due to insufficient computing power, had to compromise.

In his seminal paper, William Sharpe, who along with Markowitz would later win a Nobel Prize for their work on MPT, explains this when he admits (albeit in an obscure footnote hidden deep in the article) "Under certain circumstances, the mean-variance approach can be shown to lead to unsatisfactory predictions of behavior. Markowitz suggests that a model based on the semi-variance would be preferable;

in light of the formidable computational problems, however, he bases his analysis on the variance and standard deviation." (Sharpe, W.F., *Capital Asset Prices: A Theory of Market Equilibrium under Considerations of Risk*, The Journal of Finance, Volume 19, Issue 3, September 1964, 425-42)

Soon thereafter, standard deviation (or "volatility") became the universal measure of "risk." Eventually, it found its way in those portfolio optimization programs we mentioned elsewhere in this book. You remember. Those are the ones they use to determine a recommended asset allocation. Are you starting to connect the dots here? Do you begin to see why so much of what we see in the financial industry is defective? It's because academia and industry have constructed the main apparati (happy, Latin lovers?) based on a compromised theory.

Eventually, the world (and the computer industry) caught up to Sharpe's footnote and Markowitz's lament. Not only couldn't MPT explain regularly occurring "anomalies," but computer power eventually allowed a new generation of finance professors to try what Markowitz originally intended. But by then it was too late. MPT had too many holes in it, and researchers began a desperate search for a new theory to fill these holes. In the meantime, the use of standard deviation to represent risk has become the poster-child for all that was wrong with MPT.

APPENDIX V.
THE CHILD IRA — A SOLUTION TO THE INEVITABLE SOCIAL SECURITY CRISIS?

This may sound like an April Fools' joke, but, trust me, it's not. That's just how unbelievable it is. It's the kind of *eureka!* discovery that can only occur in the wee small hours of the morning after endlessly toiling away at numbers and statistics and statistics and numbers.

And the beauty of it is that it works!

What if I told you there was a low cost way to wipe out the need for Social Security within one generation — and not only would it not cost the government dime but it would generate massively more tax revenue. Would you believe me? Or would you call me an April Fool?

Most folks would bet on the latter — and most folks would be wrong!

It's so simple and obvious, it's amazing no one has ever thought of it before. Heck, it's such a great idea, I'm even willing to concede the debate on whether there's really a retirement "crisis." Here's how the idea first struck me…

It was while writing an article that is the basis for Chapter Twenty: How to Retire a Millionaire (Hint: It's Easier Than You Think) that the idea hit me like a ton of bricks.

There I was, playing with numbers in my spreadsheet models when, like a chemist whose accidental spill leads to the discovery of a fabulous cure, I inadvertently started at year 0 instead of year 15. (You'll have to read the Chapter to understand the significance of starting at year 15.) Curiosity getting the better of me, rather than correcting the error, I extrapolated upon it.

Lo! And Behold! came the answer that is guaranteed to solve our nation's alleged retirement crisis. OK, OK, I said I was willing to concede the point that there really is a retirement crisis. And, admittedly so, if you consider Social Security a component of retirement, then, sooner or later, like any other Ponzi Scheme, we will find ourselves in a crisis. Only, the thing is, this idea allows Social Security to die a natural death, wiping away forever our mournful addiction to this gangster era racket.

Ready?

Here's the idea.

I'll call it the "Child IRA." It's actually something a few elite folks can take advantage of now, assuming their children have been modeling since before they could crawl. Its effect — without the tax-deferred benefits — can also be duplicated today, mainly via trust funds (namely, RIC-E trusts) but also through regular investment accounts.

But what I'm proposing is not at all like these. It's a tax-deferred account that doesn't require earned income on the part of the primary beneficiary (i.e., the "Child" of the Child IRA). It would allow any adult (parents, grandparents or any other random unrelated adult for that matter) to contribute an aggregate total of $1,000 (pre-tax) to any child every year until they reach the age of 19.

Here's how it works. Every child born in the U. S. of A. would be allowed to accept up to $1,000 per year until their nineteenth birthday into their own "Child IRA." Any adult can make a tax-deductible contribution into anyone's Child IRA, so long as the total contributions to any single Child IRA do not exceed $1,000. The contributing adult does not have to be related to the child that owns the Child IRA.

Now, are you listening? Here's the beauty of the plan. All Child-IRA's would be required to be invested in long-term equities (preferably not through any government fund but through existing private investment vehicles like mutual funds). They'll be none of this "risk aversion" stuff because you can't withdraw from a Child IRA until Age 70 (the "real" retirement age by the time today's kids get there). With this kind of requirement, we'd expect these Child-IRAs to grow at the rate of return of stocks. Historically, that's a tad under 10%, but let's be conservative and say it's 8%. Do you know what that means?

That means, by contributing $1,000 a year from the year of birth until the 19th birthday (a total of $19,000 in contributions), a Child-IRA will be worth in excess of $2.2 million when the owner retires at age seventy. That's on top of any other retirement savings that person might have. And with that $2.2 million head start, where is the need for Social Security?

And what a head start it is!

The Child IRA. It's the answer to all our retirement woes. It obviates the need for Social Security (at least that part that deals with retirement). It doesn't cost the government anything to implement. Best yet, it'll leave the government with an ongoing tax windfall.

Here's how:

According to the US Census, there are roughly 75 million children in the United States. If all Child IRAs are fully funded each year, that would defer taxable income by $75 billion. Another way of saying, based on the Tax Policy Center's average Federal tax rate of 17.4 (for 2009, the latest year available), this would equate to a short-term loss of $13 billion in revenues per year. By eerie coincidence, according to the President's newly released budget, it costs a little more than $12 billion dollars to operate Social Security.

But let's not get ahead of ourselves. I said this wouldn't cost anything and here's why. Looking at the costs in another way, a fully funded Child IRA ($1,000 per year until that child's nineteenth birthday) would require a total of $19,000 in total tax deductible contributions. Again, assuming the average 17.4% tax rate, this reduces tax revenues by $174 per year for a total reduction of $3,306 over the nineteen years contributions are allowed.

By Age 70, when the child retires, assuming an average annual return of 8% (versus the historic average annual return for equities of 10.4%), the Child IRA would be worth $2,212,655. Furthermore, if the retiree now takes out 4% a year ($88,506) and pays the current average tax of 17.4%, the government will earn $15,400 in tax revenues a year. That's nearly a 9,000% return on that $174 annual "investment" the government makes during the contribution period of the Child IRA. Not bad for doing nothing.

Finally, that $88,506 is 72% more than the current median income of $51,371. Traditional retirement savings vehicles will still be needed because, like Social Security, the Child IRA is not intended to fully fund retirement.

But, unlike Social Security, the Child IRA isn't a Ponzi Scheme, doesn't cost the government money (moreover, by eliminating the annual operating cost of Social Security, it'll save the government money), and, in fact, it will increase government revenues.

Like I said, it's so obviously simple, why hasn't anyone ever come up with it before?

INDEX:

ABOUT THE AUTHOR

You might recognize Christopher Carosa as the oft-quoted President of the Bullfinch Fund and its investment adviser Carosa Stanton Asset Management, LLC. A popular and entertaining, nationally-recognized speaker from coast to coast, he has appeared in, among other media outlets, *The New York Times*, *Barron's*, CNN and Fox Business News.

In 2009, he created *FiduciaryNews.com*, an on-line news site dedicated to providing "essential information, blunt commentary and practical examples for ERISA/401k fiduciaries, individual trustees and professional fiduciaries." He serves as Chief Contributing Editor for the site, which in its first five years has seen more than half a million page views.

A prolific and provocative writer, Mr. Carosa has penned four other books: *A Pizza The Action* (Pandamensional Solutions, 2014), *401 Fiduciary Solutions* (Pandamensional Solutions, Inc., 2012); *A Life Full of Wonder* (an unpublished novel written in 2005); and, *Due Diligence* (ARDMAN Regional, Ltd., 1999). He's also written two stage plays: *Gangsters in Love* (2011) and *The Macaroni Kid* (2007). In addition to other publications, he has written more than 500 articles for various on-line and print media outlets.

A rare breed among financial journalists, Mr. Carosa has accumulated a long, variegated, and successful record as a practitioner in the financial services industry. After earning a degree in physics and astronomy from Yale University in 1982, he joined Manning & Napier Advisers, Inc. During his 14 years there, he helped start the firm's proprietary mutual fund series, created the firms custodial operations division, and created their trust company that accumulated nearly $1 billion in assets before he left. He has earned an MBA from the Simon School at the University of Rochester and the CTFA (Certified Trust and Financial Adviser) professional designation from the Institute of Certified Bankers. Today, Mr. Carosa is president of Carosa Stanton Asset Management, LLC, a boutique investment firm. He's also Chairman of the Board and President of Bullfinch Fund, Inc. a series of flexible no-load mutual funds, including one that concentrates its investments in Western New York companies.

If you'd like to read more by Mr. Carosa, feel free to browse his author's site, ChrisCarosa.com; LifetimeDreamGuide.com, a site to another book he's working on; his site devoted to his first love, AstronomyTop100.com; and, a site where he, his son, and his daughter offer reviews to classic Hollywood movies, MightyMovieMoments.com.

Mr. Carosa lives in Mendon, NY with his wife, Betsy, three children, Cesidia, Catarina, and Peter, and their beagle, Wally.

Made in the USA
Lexington, KY
22 March 2018